I'm Tryi

MW00463634

A Memoir of Love, Loss, and Misadventure

Lorraine, thanks for the interview. This was awesome. I hope you have a blast in Dallas. & I hope you enjoy my words.

October 30, 2015

By: Taylor Church

To Bonnie and Steve, the best couple I've ever known

Acknowledgments

This book would never have come to fruition if it were not for the assistance of those who are more talented than I. I only allowed a select few to read my words before publication, and even fewer were allowed to give me feedback. Being my first book, everything I wrote I loved, it was my baby. But I also hated everything I wrote, for I feared it wasn't good enough. As most authors will discover, your writing usually falls precariously into a hazy area between hubris and self-loathing. But even this discovery would have been impossible without the help of a few choice people. My Dad, who not only is extremely well read, but thinks more like me than anyone else I know. I must thank my beautiful mother, who could not stand to criticize much more than an omitted comma within my manuscript. A special thanks to my grammarian sister Brittany, who did a lot of editing and supplied my manuscript with more smiley faces than anyone else. Thanks must also be accredited to Lydia Ripplinger and Emily Fairchild for their insights into the English language and for their keen ability to find syntactical errors. I must also thank Mandi Call, who was often at my side while I typed, and who demanded to be the first to read the finished product. Helpful feedback was also given by my cousin Dallas Hawks and my younger sister Danielle. Additional and invaluable assistance was supplied by Stephanie Ottehenning. My cover would have remained unprofessional and utterly unexcellent if it were not for her expertise.

Preface

It is worth mentioning that the names of all the girls in this memoir have been changed to protect their respective identities. But it's also done to protect me from the inevitable flak I would receive if any of them ever actually read this.

Everything you read is unabashed truth. Some trivial details have been altered where memory has failed me. All conversations and quotes are accurate, though unlikely to be reproduced verbatim. This is my story, but I believe in every story we can find a little bit of ourselves.

Ch. 1 Slikowski

"Love is an exploding cigar we willingly smoke." ~ Lynda
Barry

All prepubescent romances and lesser paramours aside, I was not really affected by women until she came along. I am referring to the dreaded Slikowski. No, I was not dating a girl with the first name Slikowski. I have made a fairly juvenile habit of paying homage to my exes by entirely eliminating their first names from my vernacular. This practice makes me feel a smidge of post-jilted superiority, all the while making the girls involved feel more like they just scored a goal in P.E. class, and less like princesses made to be coddled and courted, and this is my unabashedly cruel intention.

Slikowski had me dangerously hooked from the onset. She had dark hair that flowed down near her buttocks (which is a whole other source of neurotic commentary, that I will not indulge in at this juncture), and the kind of tan that was clearly not from the sun, but not so orange as to resemble a Willy Wonka employee. She was the kind of girl I had always dreamed of meeting, despite how nauseating that sounds. We met when she was nineteen and I was twenty-two. Her inability to legally consume alcohol should have been a red flag, even though I myself was not a drinker. It would take me years to realize that a girl so close, so freshly departed from high school and her parents warm snuggly nest was usually incapable of the type of commitment and maturity I was looking for. Not that I was a beacon of maturity and/or commitment myself, but is it a crime to have unfair and ridiculous expectations? I wanted a girl that had betrothals and wedding cakes in her thoughts, not a girl that still fixated on erstwhile lovers and under-the-bleachers rendezvous.

I found out quickly with an uncomfortable amount of prying that Slikowski was not dreaming of nuptials. She was in fact pining over unrequited love from high school and trying her hardest to date me without actually dating me. I found it to be quite the paradox, but apparently, exclusivity was a very gray area, about as understandable and clear cut as C-SPAN jargon is to a nine year-old. Should I have headed for greener pastures? Should I have chalked it up as a non-victory and said adieu? Of course I should have. But instead I held even tighter to the rope that burned my hands. I was not afraid of being alone at twenty-three; I was afraid, or rather paralyzed, by the idea of losing the girl that I never thought I could obtain in the first place. How frightening is it to come out with a sophomore release when your first album is a record-breaking sensation? It's a lot of pressure, and I was terrified I could not reproduce a platinum girl like Slikowski. I was in too deep. I had learned all of the sometimes annoying idiosyncrasies of a person that ultimately endears them to you, especially if you are a sappy romantic. I had discovered myriad things about the opposite sex that ruthlessly I had never been taught or been savvy enough to pick up on by myself. I learned that women (at least this one) named their breasts. Though I thought this ritualistic naming of body parts was a rite reserved for men, I found it absurdly enthralling. I obtusely learned that women are creatures of a fastidious nature. They may be willing and capable of change, but it is not going to be because you want them to, and it certainly will not be on your uneducated terms. I found out that there was no secret elixir that would elicit a full knowledge of women. I discovered the inescapable truth that the female is an ineffable, unpredictable, beautiful, painfully frustrating, and a fascinating mystery. I will say about women what Winston Churchill said about the vast and unknown lands of Russia: (they are) "a riddle wrapped in a mystery inside an enigma." I was learning things about women I never knew before, and I romanticized the fact that I happened to be spending time with the girl that was teaching me these forbidden truths.

Despite my verbalized wishes, we were not in the type of relationship that would be defined by the suppressing and shackling terms of boyfriend and girlfriend. We occasionally saw other people, and frequented restaurants and ice-skating rinks with members of the opposite sex. But there was an untoward bylaw in our agreement that I had completely overlooked. Apparently we were allowed to go out with other people, but hooking up with said people was strictly verboten and subject to draconian punishments. This whimsical rule-making that I had no say or control over was just another red flag in what would become a quotidian parade of large and painfully crimson flags that were loudly marched in front of my house while I tried to ignore them and go back to sleep.

Time moved on as it tends to do and I convinced myself that I was happy, and that the relationship just needed time and maybe a little water. She even met my family. She became close with my sisters and things seemed to be moving in a direction that would eventually make me a felicitous man, maybe even a groom.

Then she broke up with me. I mention it so casually to show you how abruptly and almost nonchalantly Slikowski made it known to me that she no longer wanted me in her life.

Here comes the injurious irony: She absolutely still wanted me in her life. She insisted on not being my girlfriend, but could not find a way to go through life without me being in it. While I was weeping alone in my bed and listening to overplayed pop songs about anguish and betrayal, she was gleefully going about her life, while still trying to communicate with me on a daily basis.

The invention of text messaging has made breaking up, an already far from innocuous process, a deleterious and dragged-out fist fight. It is much easier to send an ill-advised text with some mawkish content like "I miss you," or the subtler "How are you?" than to pick up the phone and generate a real conversation with someone that likely does not want to speak to you. So, just when you think you are out of the pesky woods, having gone four or five days without communication, you receive a schmaltzy text, immediately thrusting you back into that self-deprecating pool of sadness you thought you had just climbed out of. Soon this cyclical concourse of events breaks you down. You know the texting is unhealthy, and that despite all of her pally texts she does not want to get back together, she just does not want to lose you altogether. This harsh realization comes and goes like the fickle precipitation of February. But denial does not last; you know the veracity of the matter. You know it is over, and that she will never care about you like you care about her. These truths are only homologated by the indie alternative songs that endlessly seep through your headphones into your fragile ears hour after hour, day after day.

For several months we would engage in seemingly harmless banter that would in turn become harmful time spent together. We would euphemistically say that we were just hanging out, just being friends. What is wrong with being friends? Then the tides would unexpectedly come in and our masquerade would be disrupted. We would kiss, blaming the time apart and the furious hormones that raged within us. I tried assiduously not to be a naïf, but to accept that the future was precarious at best. I attempted to remain cavalier and apathetic, but I was fooling no one. I wanted more than anything to get back together. I could not take any more nights of amorous ambiguity. I could not handle the three days on, four days off, as if our relationship was a part-time job at Home Depot. I demanded answers. Okay, I demanded answers in a non-verbal, passive aggressive sort of way that I hoped would telepathically alter the paradigm of the woman that was making me bonkers.

The unspoken whispers of my psyche somehow remained unheard. Slikowski could not be swayed by any amount of hoping and wishing on my part. I had to devise a plan. I had to put an end to the saga that was depriving me of sleep and any real semblance of sanity. I was sick of being hoodwinked by my leaping stomach for half a second every time I received a text from someone with her same first name. I even changed certain contacts in my phone to avoid such blunders. Her contact remained the same, though I shuddered every time it appeared on my phone.

My plan was not epic; it was desperate. I first consulted with my friends, hoping to find an undiscovered nugget of wisdom or reason. I found no such thing. The two pieces of advice I received were astonishingly unhelpful. The first one, "Screw her bro" had its definite poetic advantages. The second piece of unmitigated sagacity was, "I don't know, go talk to her or something." I found the second argument intriguing despite its obvious lack of romance and flowery verbiage.

I put on what I erroneously thought to be my best shirt at the time, summoned some hibernating courage, and called Slikowski. My brevity was praiseworthy. I simply told her that we needed to talk, and that it had to be that night. She complied, and we agreed to meet at her place and go for a drive. The unsettling nature of these rides was implicit, at least to me. I prayed for strength and a glib smoothness to be present in our confabulation, which I truly feared. I did not know if I was going to foolishly profess my love to Slikowski or if I was going to burst into a mess of unattractive tears. Other sinister alternatives circumvented my thoughts until I arrived at her apartment. We got into her blue Mazda and took off as was our custom, for she had what was apparently the superior and more appropriate means of transportation. We pumped through the platitudes that accompany awkward silence and portending confrontation all the way to our destination, an empty secluded parking lot across from a garish community park.

This was the moment that had left me uneasy and frightened in my premeditations. Though what I had wanted to say was somewhat scripted, it came out in an onslaught of superlatives and surfeited compliments. I was just trying to explain how I felt, how important she was to me, how special and prodigious I thought she was. I was fighting back that inevitable choking in your throat when crying is knocking at your windpipe. I was fighting the urges to weep and throw my arms around her when suddenly she began to speak. She explained her perpetual confusion and lack of certainty, and then *she* started to cry. I was almost chagrined. I was supposed to be the one in shambles here; I was the one that was battling unrequited emotions. I knew this was at least semi-monumental because she was not a weeper. She was never over-sentimental, and usually expressed her saccharine feelings with the word "aw," though she was rarely in an actual state of awe.

Like an experienced hunter I viewed the tender fragility of my prey and knew that its limb had been wounded. She was falling, losing blood and would soon be made into some sort of jerky. I touched her hand, and she looked at me in a way that only men can understand. No man has ever looked at a woman like this. Only a woman could give you a look that terrifyingly screams loud pitches of insecurity, lust, and the need to be kissed. Not a gentle congenial kiss of gratitude or affection, but a passionate meeting of the lips that can say more than any Shakespearean dialogue is capable of articulating. Only a completely fatuous individual would wait more than a second to attack after a glance like that. I am no such individual.

One never seems to recall how long kisses like this last. They could be twenty, thirty seconds, or three minutes. The idea of time and anything else for that matter has at this point gone on a distant walkabout. The apogee of this lippy intersection seemed to last the entire duration of the kiss. In that moment I knew that we would get back together, and that all would be blissfully glorious and unparalleled in the documented history of romance. I was wrong. After the kiss that I thought spoke volumes of things to come, it was decided that she would take the weekend, during which she would be out of town, to think things over. This sounded like an asinine idea, but I acquiesced, seeing no another pleasant alternative.

The next few days I made a point not to text her, or even think about her. That does not necessarily mean that I succeeded, but what a lofty goal it was. The day came that she was back in town and I stipulated that our conversation needed to happen post haste. She rang, and told me she would come over later that night for our little discussion.

Slikowski arrived in a less than punctual manner and we entered my bedroom without a pointless charade of pleasantries. I could sense that she was not about to implode with jubilee, but I brushed that notion aside. She sat on my bed and her finely-toned legs, molded by years of dancing, stared at me through the helpless denim of her jeans. She beseeched me at once, telling me to recount my points from our previous encounter. I felt frustratingly importuned, but once again I allowed the request. I breezed through my salient points, this time not able to hold back my tears. The tears came because I saw what she was doing. She was buying time; she did not want to outwardly tell me it was over, that I was not the one. But I wasn't. Our time in the sun had expired. The sad part was Slikowski had been much more cognizant of this gradual expiration than I. I was blindsided by my own naivety, and that hurt. She cried. I cried. And then I asked her to never under any circumstance communicate with me again. There was no malady in my voice, but I wanted my words to be clear. I could not handle seeing her again, and I knew getting over her would be a colossal assignment if we tried in any way to remain chummy.

I do not know that I loved her, but I certainly felt like I did. But who knows what love is anyways? I was pretty sure I loved Hillary Kingman, my Kindergarten crush, but I know now that that was nothing more than my first realization that I liked girls. Fast forward five years to the fourth grade and my first girlfriend Danielle Whitman. I thought love had really arrived, this time in a shiny and unmistakable package. I even blurted out a proclamation of this so-called love one time on the telephone before quickly saying goodbye and hanging up; but that too was far from actual love. Maybe it is impossible to ascertain what is and isn't love until it has come and gone. Or maybe you cannot be certain of love unless it is true love. Either way, I am not Aphrodite and suffice it to say, I did not know how I felt concerning this issue of love.

We embraced for the last time and I felt a new kind of lowness, a unique pain that I had never before had the displeasure of meeting. She welled up with tears and left. I don't know where she went, what she was thinking or if she was feeling as broken and mangled as I was. At least the difficult part was over.

The weeks stacked up and I valiantly tried to forget the existence of a person that had consumed my world for the last eight months. I did what I thought was a decent job of moving on. I went on dates. I kissed girls and repeatedly listened to music that made me quiver with melancholy. But you cannot just eliminate music from your life, can you? It is not my fault that every musician in the history of recorded music knew the intimate details and inner workings of my failed relationship. I do not remember contacting bands and relaying my tragedy to them, so they could exploit my sadness: yet, somehow they were all keenly aware of my struggle. I couldn't tell if the songs had an underlining tone of debauchery or if they were romantic tributes in honor of unrequited love.

At any rate, I could not escape the lyrics of lovers and the sight of ambivalent love on the streets. It's funny how your personal catastrophe often has little effect on the outside world. People continue to frolic about, unaware of your despondency.

But I was fine. Sure, I hurt. Sure, I had trouble sleeping. Sure, I wondered how I would recover from the recent dismantling of my heart. But I was fine. Life would move on and I would gladly be a part of it. My Dad in his infinite wisdom explained to me that my future wife would be even hotter. I was not positive this was true. Maybe she would be a different type of hot. Maybe blonder, maybe a smaller waist? Maybe she would not tell me to stop biting my fingernails. Perhaps she would not pester me about standing up straight. Slikowski used to always ask me in her impetuous kindergarten teacher voice, "How tall are you Taylor?" as if that condescending remark would remind me that my slouching was unacceptable. Maybe my future bride would hold my hand in fricking public.

Although I did not see it at the time, my Dad's words rang true and glorious like the Magna Carta. I started realizing that I was never dating a perfect person. It is hard to tell if it is embitterment or hindsight that causes you to recall all the faults and flaws of your ex, but it is a beautiful and cathartic process. It may not be the most

salubrious practicum, but it is better than pining over the smell of her

hair, or re-reading an especially tender text message. These things

are unhealthy. Mudslinging and crafty slandering was the only

normal way I could think of to move on, and I yearned for normalcy.

Ch.2 Lilly Part I

"A man in love mistakes a pimple for a dimple." ~ Japanese

Proverb

I know I said that girls who have entered my life and acrimoniously exited would be heretofore referred to by surnames. But this one was different. I never got to the point where I could do that with her. I am not sure why. I guess she had somewhat of a lugubrious trance over me, and for better or worse I could not bring myself to do anything that was in the least bit degrading to her. But we will discuss the narcissistic deification of her in a little bit.

A month or so after the Slikowski debacle, my overly gregarious friend Michael and his spacey girlfriend Kassandra set me up on a blind date. Normally I find the idea of blind dates to be a repugnant waste of time reserved for the uncouth and asocial types of people. But Kassandra had found me charming and quite suitable, so she thought I would be perfect for her friend. Michael was just the liaison, and feeling somewhat flattered and still chopfallen I agreed to this blind date with a one condition. I would require her name so I could properly stalk her on all forms of social media. I am well aware that most women find all of their friends to be cute, and they all seem to have sparkling personalities to go along with their putative beauty. So, I had to be wary. I looked her up on Facebook and found her to be swanky with a comely face and an interesting look to her. I agreed to rendezvous.

I was ordered to message her and form a date on my own accord. So, I sent her a witty message online and awaited her enthusiastic response. I was neither giddy nor discouraged about the whole thing. My giddiness had recently fled, and I was surviving just a few notches above apathy. The next day I received a perky message on Facebook from my upcoming date, stating that she would love to get together sometime. She complimented my verbiage and supplied me with her phone number. This bumped me to the next notch of emotional stability that still lay somewhere between indifference and excitement.

Over the next couple of days we participated in the required dalliance of flirtatious, playful and strategic texts, a sort of non-verbal warm-up to our scheduled outing. On Thursday I was studying in the library when I got a phone call from the girl that will now be called Lilly. I answered a little bemused, since the plan was for me to call her the following day to confirm our meeting. Turns out she had dialed me by mistake in an attempt to send a text. Her nervous confession coupled with her delicate voice twisted a knot in my stomach almost foretelling a future of felicity and good fortune. It was as if I had swallowed a fortune cookie and now understood and believed its cosmic power to produce good luck. Our skittish conversation stretched on for several minutes, as we both realized we enjoyed whatever was on the other side of that telephone.

That Friday night it was time. I had been on plenty of post-Slikowski dates, and had my share of amorous, if ill-advised nights, but this was perhaps the first date I was actually apprehensive about. I drove to her apartment on the West side of town and walked up to the third floor, not knowing what to expect. Women have a way of either being wonderfully photogenic or horrifically deceiving; especially with the photo editing that is available now. She opened the door and hurled a smile in my direction. I fumbled with it, but caught it and found myself looking at her up and down. She wore a black top with colorful circles throughout that looked like Froot Loops. She invited me in for a mini tour of the place, but more likely to shake off the palpable nerves that she had. I had them too. I saw a piano in the living room and remembered that she had told me she was a musician of sorts. In what I thought was a jocular tone, I asked her if she would play something for me. The request must have exited my mouth in a more somber and curious tone than I realized because she confidently obliged and asked me what I wanted to hear. Unprepared, I asked if she would play me an original. I was not prepared for what happened next. She starting palpating the ivories and her voice erupted. I don't recall the lyrics or length of the song, I just know at that moment she had me. It was not just her skill that captivated me, but her voice, a melodic and gorgeous utterance. She obviously knew how to play the game. She had put me in checkmate before I had a chance to give my pawns a pep-talk.

Our internet-era meet cute had left me bereft of logic and reason. Whatever game plan I had carelessly put in my head beforehand was gone, and was not going to be writing me encouraging postcards from wherever it fled to. Before we proceed to dinner, let me paint you a picture of this dame. Lilly was petite, maybe 5'4". She could not have topped the scales at any more than one hundred pounds. But honestly I have no idea how much girls weigh, never have. Regardless, she was skinny. And since I am no porterhouse myself, I prefer my partners to be slender fillets. Despite her slim, even tiny figure she managed to be extremely busty. I suspected that she had had a friendly visit with a cosmetic surgeon at some point, but I would find out later that this was not the case. Her skin was perfect, only blemished by the occasional archipelago of freckles that actually added to her mystique. Her hair was long and brown. Her face could not be viewed without noticing her eyes; they were fresh water reservoirs that clearly had an unknown depth to them. I am not sure where she got her waist, but it was smaller than anatomy would usually assign anyone. She was a little piece of artistic genius, and she seemed very excited to go out with me. The sagacious thing to do in these situations is to not overanalyze the data, but to simply count yourself lucky. So, that's what I did.

We arrived at the restaurant where I ordered a burrito the size of a marsupial. Lilly ordered a fancy salad. The food was music in the background. We ate because we were in a place of victuals, and because it was dinner time. But the task of masticating, sipping, and swallowing was all secondary to our colloquy. We were both so engaged in one another, and in each other's responses that we barely made sense of what we were saying. Smiles reigned supreme, and it was decided that we would return to her apartment to watch a movie.

A normal choice for a first date screenplay would be a light romantic comedy or perhaps a frightening film that would elicit the necessity of cuddling. We went another route. We decided to watch a three and a half hour depressing and violent epic, *Schindler's List*. What could possibly compel me to suggest such a movie? Was I mad? Did I somehow think this was a movie about a charming protagonist that made cute lists for his lover? No. Lilly had mentioned during dinner that she had never seen it and had always wanted to. I quickly, without calculating its implications, suggested that we go rent the film. I warned her that it was macabre and extremely lengthy, but her enthusiasm did not wane. So, we rented it and returned to her abode.

The time it takes to put in the DVD, turn the TV to the correct input and fast forward through the previews, possibly prepare popcorn and drinks, and decide on appropriate seating arrangements and temperature levels is entirely too much time for the mind to preoccupy itself with absurd concerns and unlikely scenarios. What if my breath is sub-par? What if we watch an entire movie without bodily contact? What if she wants me to kiss her? I wouldn't want us to miss key cinematic plot points. What if she wants me to hold her hand but I am too cowardly? Luckily a rapid fast-forward option only gave me about a minute or so to panic.

Having obvious home court advantage, she decided which couch would seat us and what amount of blankets would accompany us. The movie commenced and my nerves fled, but my wondering thoughts persisted. Does she think this movie is too long? Too boring? Does she want me to scoot in a little closer? So, I played it cool. I remained proximate, but with the most minimal amount of touching. As the film progressed, so did I. Soon we were holding hands and I could feel something doing somersaults in my stomach. That three-and-a-half-hour saga seemed to breeze by, and at some point we transformed into horizontal acquaintances. I was then even more cognizant of the amazing body she possessed.

The film ended and we kept talking, kept creeping closer and closer to each other. Oxygen was not important; heat was important.

Touching was important. We mutually agreed that the neighboring couch would suit us better, so we moved. It was getting late. We were becoming somnolent. But I had to kiss her. We had come as close as you can come to kissing someone without actually kissing them; a sort of confab that consisted of subtle lip grazes and deep breaths and very idle and forgettable chatter. After this frustrating and intoxicating tango, I summoned up the courage and proceeded all the way to her soft lips. Her mouth reacted with surprise and pleasure. We kissed for some time. Was it magical? Did my heart burst into pixy dust? No. Honestly, I had had better and was marginally disappointed. It wasn't that she was a bad kisser. She was good. I simply and superficially found her mouth to be too small. The kiss lacked a certain French aspect that I hoped for. Maybe I was being too shallow, or maybe it was 5:00 a.m. and I was simply too tired.

I ended up staying the night, our intimacy halting at the kissing boulevard. I woke up a little bemused, yet happy to be lying next to a beautiful girl. I went home and promised to call her. Being the cavalier serial dater that I was, I really was not sure if I would call her. But, I was intrigued by the fact that I might.

I did. I called her. We starting hanging out more frequently until one day I realized we were together every day. Things were lovely and pleasant and I found that I actually enjoyed kissing her more than anyone I had ever kissed before. Her lips were not too small, they were supple and perfect. We spent our time kissing, talking music and picking and choosing which childhood memories to retell.

Like most women, Lilly had demons looming just beneath a strategic veneer of makeup and optimism. Her oldest brother had given up the ghost when she was just a little girl. She had a beautiful mother that was loving, though hard to read and prone to fits of anxiety. On top of that she had another brother, handsome with wavy black hair who often stole the coveted spotlight of adolescence. Being a beautiful girl she naturally had crazy exes and men that had treated her poorly. These demons were not particularly apparent, but there was clearly a deep emotionality to this girl. And though it could have been viewed as a red flag, it drew me even closer to her.

As we spent more and more time together, I feared the inevitable relationship discussion. I loved spending time with her, but despite what I wanted to think, I was still healing from wounds inflicted during the Battle of Slikowski. We had only been seeing each other a couple of weeks when she sprang it on me. We were sitting on her bed talking and smooching in what I thought was a carefree moment. Well, the moment swiftly changed gears, and before I knew it I was in the middle of defending why I was not ready for exclusivity. I also was not ready to stop seeing her, so we decided that I would ponder it, and return with a more definitive answer in a few days. I had no idea what I was going to do. I never know what I am going to do.

A few days later I made a tragic mistake that I have replayed countless times in my head. It is one of those things that you paradoxically understand why you did it at the time, but you still consider it an inexcusable error. Not only did I reject her request to go steady, I did it in a terrible fashion. I had her pick me up from my house and we resumed our serious talk in her apartment. I guess I had my mind on different things, and secretly hoped I would be allotted a few more days to make my decision. So I pushed it aside, and hoped it would go away for the time being, like with a toddler incessantly asking you questions.

We casually went about our routine of chatter and making out when all things turned black. Sure enough, she remembered my deadline. With her fragile body in my arms she asked me if I would essentially be her boyfriend. I am not sure what sort of sinister malady overtook my being at that moment, but I told her in no uncertain terms that I could not make that commitment. Then as tears rushed out of her eyes something awful and mortifying happened. I started to cry. This was completely unacceptable. The breaker-upper is not supposed to weep. She asked why I was crying, and I could retort with no satisfactory or masculine answer, because I myself had no idea why I had been attacked by this pernicious and wet emotion.

We sat there in the darkness, both muted by the realization that it was all over just as quickly as it had begun. It took us longer than it should have to regain our lost composure and exit her bedroom. This upsetting sequence of events was only exacerbated by the fact that I could not leave on my own. I needed a ride. Amateur move. How could I break up with a girl knowing full well that a ride home alone with her was imminent? As I look back on the litany of things I should have done differently with Lilly, this particular driving logistics faux pas was not the worst of the bunch, but was still cruel and thoughtless.

We entered her little white car, both still fighting back tears the way you would when you had been humiliated at school in front of your classmates, who were your entire world. She popped in a CD to distract us both from our thoughts, and certainly from any audible communication. I am not sure if Cupid was inebriated and forgetful of his normal function, but the song that came on first could not have been more painfully apropos. The song was "Breakeven," by The Script. The song starts out innocently enough mentioning a wavering belief in deity, followed by the introduction of a relationship likely doomed. Then an ominous lyric creeps its head out of a crusty and dark cave saying "When a heart breaks, it don't break even." That lyric alone could have been brushed aside, perhaps even gone unheard, but the refrain rang loud with a silver bullet, stating "What am I supposed to say when I'm all choked up and you're ok?" Even though the lyric was not entirely analogous to our recent events, it felt excruciatingly tantamount.

Clearly and rightly upset, Lilly ejected the CD at the precise moment that the lyrics cut into her. It is amazing the amount of pain one piece of poetry, written by a complete stranger unaware of our existence, can induce within us. It's not so much the prose, but rather the truth that so often attacks us like hornets.

We finally got back to my apartment. I could feel in the air the fact that we both had already forgiven each other. The anger had subsided with eloquent rapidity, and we were left with utter sadness and looming regret. I stepped out, and she quickly opened her door, wanting a physical goodbye. I had so much to say that I said absolutely nothing. I held her tight, took in her scent and cried again. She cried, just loud enough to break my heart. I summoned the strength to let go of her perfect body, kissed her forehead and said goodbye.

I walked the fifty yards or so back to my apartment feeling completely destroyed. Tears were in my eyes, and snot was running mercilessly out of my nose, reassuring me that I was in fact a mess. My stomach ached with the notion that I may have made a mistake. I saw a tall figure headed my way and I prayed it was no one I knew. It was Bryce, my 6'5" roommate, an ever enthusiastic and loyal friend. He could not see the emasculating moisture on my face from his vantage point, so he screamed out jubilantly "What's up baby!?" I was in no mood for tomfoolery. I wanted to sulk deeper into my self-created doldrums. On the other hand, I was in desperate need of a friend. Not just a buddy, but a best friend, someone I could openly hang my head with. Bryce and I had been through battles. I had seen him cry, and this was not the first time he witnessed an emotional unraveling on my part.

I tried as hard as I could muster to greet big Bryce with a jovial jab of some sort, but I couldn't hide the recent collapse of my world. And he could see it. He saw it like any real friend would. I broke down and we embraced. I loved him for it, because I really did not need advice in that moment. I just needed someone to hug me and allow my dam to flow. And he understood that. So there we sat, two grown men on a bench surrounded by a grassy pathway covered with trees and collegiate memories. I'm sure it was a sight to see. We are always so quick to ridicule and poke fun of other people at their lowest, when we have no ability to actually view ourselves outside of ourselves when we are at *our* lowest. But I am sure if we could step outside ourselves and stare back we would be frightened by the image, by our own wind-tossed vulnerability and weakness.

I soon returned to a less tearful and fragile disposition and decided to go visit my two sisters who lived nearby. I needed a woman's point of view. I needed to hear that I was not a monster, that Lilly would get over it, and that she had no right to hate me. But strangely I wanted to hear that I was a monster, that I was not going to get over it, and that Lilly had every right to hate me, because that was the terrible truth. When you are truly hurting you want to hear two things. You want to hear the truth, but you also want to hear something that will make you feel less sick and terrible inside. It's a twisted paradox, and puts those around you in a difficult spot. My sisters were annoyingly predictable; they did everything that sisters are supposed to do. They sided with me, cried with me and made me cookies. Even though the warm eulogies and treats made me feel better, there was still an enormous disquiet deep inside of me. I knew I was not a monster, but I had acted like one. I had been perilously running on top of a fence for weeks and finally fell, but it was clear now that I had fallen on the wrong side. I didn't fall into the yard with freshly cut grass and a steaming Jacuzzi. No, I fell into the grungy pit that masqueraded as a backyard, but was in reality a diseased hole of squalor and insidious parasites. What had I done? Was this irreparable? Could I get out of this black ditch and back over the fence to the other side? Would I ever see Lilly again? I started to aggressively worry. This is precisely when I received a text message from the freshly jilted.

As I already knew from my interlude with Slikowski, breakups these days have a very nebulous sense of finality. They are trademarked by unexpected post scripts and ill-advised texts. I may not run into my once significant other in my daily routine, but pictures and videos of them and their activities are readily and painfully available with the click of a mouse. Even deleting ex-lovers from various social media accounts doesn't punctuate the failed courtship, for I can still view their profiles as often as my loneliness permits. OK, maybe I would be one of the unfortunate ones that got cruelly blocked on Facebook or Instagram. Even then in this tragic instance one can wallow over a girl and her perfectly edited photographs by getting on a friend's computer or phone. How am I supposed to cut ties? How am I supposed to move on? Who has the time or means to renounce technology and move to Tibet every time a relationship grows sour?

This inability our culture has created to estrange ourselves from one another in the wake of a break-up had finally worked in my favor. I had broken up with a girl that I did not want to break up with. I had made a mistake, and was too proud to drive back to her place and declare my idiocy. So a post-script text that ached of hope and despair was exactly what I was praying for.

To tell the truth I didn't expect such a sudden act of disparity on her part, but as I profusely checked my pockets for any semblance of buzzing, I found that Lilly had texted me. This was too much. There was no way I could handle the contents of that message. Or perhaps it was a touching message of wonder and forgiveness. While remaining within their sight I immediately withdrew myself from my sisters and devoured the incoming text messages. Lilly had reached out to tell me that she still cared for me and that despite what had just transpired she thought I was an amazing guy, and that I deserved the best. I certainly did not deserve the best, but who was I to give spoiler alerts at this point? Despite not being particularly knowledgeable about sports, she had clearly devised a strategic Hail Mary. I was still imbued with a mysterious and distasteful reluctance, but I was starting to feel like her last ditch effort might work. I was a frightened cornerback that had gotten beat deep, and my forthcoming capitulation was evident.

We texted back and forth until the wee hours of the night, revealing to each other things that would be severely embarrassing if read by anyone else. She told me that she had never felt *that way* about a guy, so quickly in her life. I admitted that though I had never said it to her or anyone else, what I was feeling was the closest thing to being in love I had ever felt. This sounds like an agonizingly low budget made-for-TV-movie-romance, but it felt like what I was going through would receive some serious Oscar buzz.

After a day or two of regret and text exchanges that reeked of pathos, we both decided we had made a huge mistake. And when I say both, I mean me. Lilly was just too good of a person to hurl all the deplorable blame on me. We reunited and it was beautiful. Her face seemed to illustrate to me that I had made the right choice in crawling back. She donned a smile with a twofold message: first, I am so glad you are back, and when I am with you the rest of the universe becomes but a blur in the background, and secondly, if you betray me again I will be gone forever. Imagine the menacing feelings her duplicitous grin thrust upon me. She was clearly in charge, and her aggressive lack of predictability scared me greatly. But I was in no position to make demands.

A week later I made a demand. Lilly was so hell-bent on this immediate notion of exclusivity and ultimatums that I felt I had a modicum of wiggle room for requests. I don't actually believe I was right in my thinking, but it worked. For about one day. After yet another conversation about the future of our relationship, I proposed a compromise. I mentioned that during our courting interim I had agreed to take a certain girl out, and that I felt obligated to follow through. She said she too had a blind date she was planning to go on. To this day I don't believe she actually had a date planned for that Friday, but that is hardly the point. I suggested that we take the week to really think long and hard about what we wanted, go on our respective dates and reconvene Saturday for a final verdict. She complied, and it was settled. She had one condition to this deal, and it was clearly based on ugly premonitions. She said "You are not going to kiss her are you?" I retorted swiftly with a hint of offense, as if this was an absurd outrage of a possibility. She reminded me that I had kissed her on our first date, so it did not seem that farfetched. She was always full of quips that could only be defended by begrudged mutterings of the word touché. So, I agreed that there would be no smooching, no hanky-panky, and nothing but a meal and friendly, platonic banter.

What I most certainly omitted in this historic conversation with Lilly was that I had wanted to go out with my Friday-Night Girl for years. I had met Summers two summers ago in Delaware at a bowling alley. I was working in Philadelphia, and had met up with some friends one night in a dirty old bowling alley in Newark, rocking my best button-up tee. Summers was appropriately named. She exuded vitamin D, and her skin looked like it was airbrushed. She was the perfect color and her complexion rather stupefied me. I was not terribly smitten at first, because I knew at the end of the summer I was moving back to Utah, and she was staying in Delaware to finish school. We exchanged numbers and kept in relative contact. About a year later during one of my forced Slikowski hiatuses I had run into Summers in a club in Salt Lake City. It was unbelievable. She had moved out to Utah for school and to be closer to her siblings. The move had nothing to do with me; in fact she did not even find it necessary to alert me of her coming west. Alas, I was excited. We spoke for a few minutes in the loud and dark room that was inflicted with bass-heavy techno songs. We agreed that we would "have to get together sometime." Well we have all heard that a thousand times haven't we? It is basically the social convention to make non-committal, tentative plans with someone you have not seen in a while upon running into them. So we followed suit and made ultra-specific plans to do some undetermined activity at an unknown time in an undisclosed location. But I remained optimistic.

As the following year passed by Summers got a serious boyfriend, and I was more or less involved with Slikowski. Right after the initial rupture with Lilly I received a text from Summers saying, "Hey, I am single we should hang out :)" I couldn't believe the timing, and I convinced myself that it was more than sickening happenstance. So, truth be told, I was ecstatic to go out with this little plum from the East Coast, but at the same time I was terrified I would like her, or much worse, kiss her.

I kissed her. Did I not learn my lesson? Did I not remember how sick I felt about hurting Lilly the first time? How obtuse and selfish can a guy be? Let's try and forget that I am a horrible person for just a second, and let's hear my side of the story. Okay, I guess there is no way to tell this story without me sounding like a complete schmendrick. Bottom line is we went to Denny's, had sparkling conversation and gobbled down fatty breakfast foods. This put us in a lethargic state, forcing us to go back to my place and watch a movie on my bed. I blame Denny's for my loneliness. But let's not get ahead of ourselves. As we all know, watching movies horizontally in the dark with someone you are attracted to is much like a coiled spring. You would have to be a devout Monk or an asexual anomaly for something amorous not to transpire amidst the beautiful soundtrack and the disheveled pillows. Turns out we were no better than the laws of nature. Giggles presided and tickling quickly turned into kissing. I couldn't help myself. Her lips were next level. They were bigger and softer than any white girl should be allowed to have on her face. And furthermore, she knew what she was doing. Although I doubt she knew the uproar she would cause the following day.

That night I went to sleep with a bemused and vacuous feeling. I knew I may have been on the cusp of something great, but I also was grievously aware of the fury I was unfurling with Lilly if I told her about Summers, whom I promised not to kiss. Despite the late hour I struggled to get more than a couple hours of peaceful rest. My conscience was repeatedly kicking me in the shins, and who knows how my conscience got a hold of cleats, but it did. Seeing

Lilly the next day hovered over me like a heavy anvil covered in spikes.

I had quickly realized that my night with Summers was likely a pyrrhic victory. It was amazing and even more than I had expected, but it would surely come at a price I could not afford. What lay before me was a question of ethics. Could I waltz into Lilly's apartment and feign that nothing happened with Summers, and that I had decided I wanted to be with her and only her? Could I be so callously mendacious? I could. It would be easy. Could one innocuous fib be that hard to tell? I convinced myself that it would be for the greater good to lie. Things would likely not work out with Summers, and despite our passionate night, she was no Lilly. So I headed to Lilly's apartment with a step of false confidence with the full intention of lying to her. I arrived and she hugged me, summoning me to her quarters for questioning. That anvil that was six feet above my head had sprouted razor blades to accompany its injurious spikes. Whatever sinister force was holding it above me was loosening its grip. I could feel it slipping. I could feel the end. I could feel the pain, and the inevitable crushing of all things.

I sat down on her bed and she wasted not a single breath. "Did you kiss her?" As those words fluttered out of her mouth I prepped the false statement in my mind and at the last second I choked on a thread of culpability. I have always been a fairly honest fellow, but I thought I could wriggle my way into a dishonest word or two to save my own fanny. I was wrong. My bloody conscience won, and I responded to Lilly's accusation with a painful and vacillating "Um, yes."

As soon as I uttered my confession I tried in vain to couple it with an explanation. That explanation however will forever go unheard like the death-bed mutterings of a man exiled and alone. Before I could get a whiff of air out of my mouth in my own defense, she raised her hand, and pointed to the door. "Get out of my apartment" she tersely spoke, without the slightest remorse. I had hurt her, and not for the first time. This time she was crying and I was nothing but dumbstruck, not with the situation but with my own stupidity. It's like I was trying new and innovative ways to remain unhappy and alone. At least I was succeeding at something.

I walked back to my car in one of those ridiculously small parking lots that requires twelve-point turns to successfully exit. I got in my car and drove back home. What could I do? If I walked back in, I would have been slapped. I had no more rope, no more resources. The only thing I could do was let go. At least that is the logical thought process. Like my tendency towards honesty, I like to think I am also a rather logical man. But when it comes to women, beautiful women at that, I am about as logical as an octopus's garden in the shade.

So, as my logic went for a walkabout and my soul seemed more and more vacant, I tried to move on. I tried to forget about my sweet Lilly. I tried to put behind me the mistakes I made and the insipid feelings that seemed to attach themselves to me like a fanny pack. And for a couple months I kind of just sauntered around. I was not depressed, but I was roaming. It's like I was searching for something in a cave with no flashlight and no idea if I was headed towards the entrance or the exit.

Ch. 3 Drifting

"I wasn't kissing her, I was whispering in her mouth." ~

Chico Marx

Like any young man in his twenties that is at least semi-attractive and has any ability to charm or swoon I went binge dating to mend my wounds. I knew no other way. My father so colorfully referred to me as a serial dater, saying I went through women like Jerry Seinfeld. He was accurate. I certainly was not at the top of the dating food-chain, but I was no neophyte, I knew what I was doing.

I was working at Payless Shoes at the time, volunteering as an assistant high school basketball coach at a local high school making the bare minimum to feed myself, pay rent, go to school and occasionally buy a girl ice-cream, not in hopes of satiating her cravings for sugar, but to surreptitiously lure her into my vortex of seduction. Ice cream seems to have a cosmic power to attract women, a simple fact they do not teach you in middle school. The same is true with chocolate.

My dating blitzkrieg started with a girl that had four years on me. This was exciting, easy and a great way for me to forget about the girl that had formed a rather permanent squatting ground in my brain. Terry was from Texas, and like most Texans it somehow was a major part of her personality. The first night we went out, we both found comfortable solace in a couch and conjoined faces. She was simple, didn't text me unless she wanted to hang out, and was not trying to court me seriously, which is what I seriously needed. We had three, maybe four nights together. Each night was nothing but a re-run with only slightly altered dialogue. But with my newly molded cavalier attitude, three or four times with one female would be categorized as special. Needless to say Terry and I had our business, and both moved on as if nothing ever happened. This is the beauty of casual hookups. Sure, they don't actually heal you or make you forget about *her*, but they are temporary doses of happiness and retreat from lingering aches. And who doesn't need that sometimes?

Next on my maniacal conquest was Fitz. Fitz was not an intelligent girl. She was an easy pick-up, and spent most of her time in tanning beds and staring at her iPhone. Our time together was if you can imagine even less romantic than it was with Ms. Texas. Fitz was a girl from southern Idaho, not the type of dreamy small town girl that exudes bucolic beauty. She was a bumpkin. Sure she was pretty, in good shape and liked to makeout, but she was not a shining moment for me. But I was not in the business of creating shining moments; I was just in the business of moments.

I would like to think that while I was kissing strange women and wandering about somewhat aimlessly that Lilly had exited my thoughts. But no. I was in a pensive pit, that no amount of girls could release me from. This captivity, however, would have no apparent effect on me. I trudged forward in an attempt to feed my own demons. And those little bastards were ravenous.

Bostwick was my next victim, though she might have enjoyed our bawdy times together more than I did, in a disturbing masochistic sort of way. My friend and I met her under false pretenses. This is how we met women: we picked an arbitrary apartment complex that housed young co-eds and proceeded to knock on doors pretending we were future tenants curious about the layout, the surrounding area, etc. We would often get invited in, and that's when the nefarious magic would happen. Bostwick caught on to our antics, but did not care. She didn't happen to have very cute roommates, so my friend and I both got her phone number. This ended in us scheduling a rendezvous for later that night. Clearly one girl and two guys isn't an ideal ratio for friendly courtship. But we were not looking for courtship. We were looking for one-night victories. And all three of us were victors that strange and memorable night.

For my own well-being I decided definitively that I would not see this girl again. She had more issues than the Middle East and most of them involved a twisted and sinister past I did not want to be a part of. So, I never saw this girl again except one more night a few weeks later, when boredom and loneliness found their cruel apogee.

A few more nymphs crept in and out of my life in a way that felt refreshing and irresponsible all at once. I was drifting. Sometimes in our damaged minds we think we can float around on driftwood and maybe find what we are looking for. In reality we all know we have to get our gear on, and go deep sea diving if we are going to find anything of true value. But for a while the cool breeze and ease of the ocean is enough. So we drift for miles, closing our eyes and hoping we will run into an exotic tropical island that will solve all of our problems. But who are we kidding? We are in the middle of the ocean, there are sharks looming just below us, and storms are likely to hurl us into the deep and unforgiving waters.

I was content to meander through life, bemused and moderately happy. Girls were my drug of choice, and as any junkie will tell you, there are many ways to mix and blend your drugs. I soon met a splendid little girl in my apartment complex that was a sunflower in a dark alley. She was a paragon of perkiness and annoying optimism. We took to each other quickly and began spending considerable amounts of time together. She was tall and had auburn hair and full lips. Let's call her Finn. Finn was great, only one problem: I did not care about her in the least. She was lovely, well-spoken and mildly cultured, but I could not for the life of me conjure up any sentiment for her. She soon realized that we were never going out, always going in, and that I was often occupied with other courters. I don't blame her. I toyed with her relentlessly, feigning true interest, but refused to commit even to a certain night of the week to rendezvous. She called it off, in search of something more serious, and I applauded her decision and wished her great success. Some women, no matter how much you enjoy them simply deserve something better, something more tangible, more ready, more sophisticated.

Rigby, my next dame, was frankly a poor decision. I don't even remember how we met, which is probably due to my non-stop woman-hunting that consumed all of my spare time. Rigby, to be polite, was not the fairest damsel I had been with. She had just made it salaciously clear that she wanted me, and that she would not require any wooing or foreplay. I was reluctant to meet up with her at first because she was a little beneath the required level of attractiveness that I thought was pretty concrete. When you are broken, however, very little in your life remains concrete. Most of the pieces that make up your life become shriveled down to an egg-shell thickness, making your every move precarious, often ending in shards and bloody hands.

Our trysts were characterized by extinguished lights and lousy makeout sessions. Rigby was nice, but we had virtually zero conversation. Our meet ups were for one purpose, to forget. The truth is when you are fanatically rebounding from one girl to another; you are still left thinking about the girl you really care about as your head hits the pillow. Sometimes there might even be another head by your pillow, but something about impending slumber makes us think about the ones that got away, the ones that have permanent real estate in our otherwise vacuous hearts. So, even just to have something else to recall as we wrestle our demons and try to count sheep, we spend meaningless time with numerous members of the opposite sex.

A few more lassies found their way into my life for brief moments while I was denying the void that Lilly had created. No matter your intentions, some people that enter into your own little world are about as noteworthy as the type of cereal you had that morning. It's just the way it is.

While I remained jaded and entangled in my own feelings of regret and loneliness, I met an amazing girl. Months had passed since the loss of Lilly, and my heart was starting to creep open like an old dusty attic door that had not been touched in years. Her name was Jackson. She was stunning in an intimidating way. She was the type of girl that came across as being completely pompous and vain, but in truth was just very pretty, and very shy, a dangerous blend.

The first night we met, I assumed she was completely disinterested in meeting me. I couldn't blame her at the time, but that did not stop me from thinking she was a terrible and arrogant person. I got courageous and maybe a little self-righteous, calling her out on her stuck-up aloofness. She profusely apologized and pleaded her case of shyness and frequently oblivious disposition.

That initial night I hated her, and then loved her. Our adjacent bodies seemed to melt into one another on the couch as our initial notions of each other evaporated. We talked until seven in the morning, when Jackson sadly revealed that she did not live in Utah. She was from Austin and was just in town visiting her best friend, who my roommate had been seeing casually. I was instantly dejected and off put by this last minute revelation. I couldn't catch a break. We promised to stay in contact, and she admitted that moving to Utah was in the realm of possibility within the coming year. It sounded hopeful and borderline romantic, but I knew better. I knew the ranchers and music aficionados of Central Texas would steal her away from me before I had a legitimate chance.

To my fickle dismay, Jackson and I continued to correspond with one another with the missives of the twenty-first century. We texted tirelessly, lovingly attacked one another's social media profiles, and even Skyped. She was simple, seemed to like me more than the usual acquaintance, and had the added bonus of being twenty-two hours away from me. Distance has a way of eliciting feelings of romance and mercurial nostalgia. We talked about being together, and explored the future while knowing it was an unlikely and far off possibility.

During the Jackson chapter I was actually forgetting about Lilly. I was terrified to contact her, and I knew she would never reach out to me, so forgetting seemed to be my only option, and Miss Jackson helped immensely with that. As Jackson remained distant, I had scattered relapses with young girls of my past. They were all girls that I simply and maliciously did not care about.

I started to move on. Jackson was a lovely future option that was on the back of my mind, and Lilly was becoming just a memory that I had hid under my floor boards so I would not return to it with any ease. I was progressing in school somewhat, and had started a new job fixing windshields. I was still drifting on my makeshift raft in the water, but I was no longer facedown and rudderless. I had created a fishing device, and gained a hope that rescue would come.

Ch. 4 Lilly Part II

"Love is a grave mental disease." ~ Plato

I thought I had moved past Lilly. But songs still talked about her, her lips could still be tasted at odd times, and my subconscious had long and grandiloquent dialogues with her. I had other girls, other things to occupy my smudgy mind, but the yearning persisted. I had to give it one last chance, and every Taylor Swift song I heard confirmed this.

I knew that Lilly had moved into a new apartment, but I was unaware of the whereabouts. This meant I could not randomly show up at her door begging for forgiveness, and I could not make any sort of romantic gesture that was not via telephone. An actual phone call was far too risky. There's no way she would answer the call, or more accurately I was petrified of what she might say if she did pick up the phone. Texting was the answer. Any verbal weaknesses I had were made up for with painstaking and devastatingly clever textual offensives. I had nothing to lose. Lilly was already gone; she could not, in my mind, become even more gone.

I stared at my phone. It laughed at me. It knew my game plan was flawed and doomed. What could I possibly say to atone for what I had done? I stopped overthinking and nervously scrolled down my contact list until I came to the L's. I found her name, that sinister name with the power to make me queasy, and then opened the message. Again my phone taunted me, making me think no medley of words or apologies could bring back the one that got away. I was offended by my Blackberry's audacious debauchery, so I started typing. I was still nervous, but I trudged forward with my apologetic prose. Despite my plans to send her a sonnet that would render her comatose, in the end I kept it simple. I told her I missed her and that I was sorry. I made it clear that I did not deserve any sort of response, but that she had the right to know I still thought about her and that I would do anything for a second chance.

After I had typed every word, checked for grammatical accuracy, and vacillated over alternative sentences and adjectives, I pressed send. In a moment like this, you want and half expect a response within thirty seconds. You forget that the person on the other end of your correspondence might not be clutching the phone awaiting a life-altering text message. They might actually be living their lives. You know this, but you fear that they saw the text and simply decided that responding or even reading it was not a pressing matter. I often bemoan the fact that I did not live in the days where jilted lovers and hopeful romantics sent and received letters. I would kill for a mushy missive full of cursive lettering and flowery confessions. Instead, I receive pithy text messages with smiley faces and superfluous letters to emphasize enthusiasm. No one would take the time to write an epistle that only said "yessss, I miss yooou, let's hang soooon!!!!"

Alas, I remained in the texting generation, so I waited for a response from my Lilly. I set my phone down on my bed and paced around my apartment pretending to do something, anything. I turned on the TV, watched a show or two without hearing a single word. There was a muted horror in the air. All I could hear were my paranoid thoughts. Was she going to text me back? Was she currently Googling how to block someone from her phone? Was she nervously composing an amorous text? My brain was having mini earthquakes, and I had no place of refuge.

About an hour later, I dashed to my phone to check my text inbox. There undisturbed laid a message from Lilly. This was the moment. I prepared myself for the worst before I opened it. Surely she would tell me what a repulsive human being I was and strip me of any manhood that remained.

The text read, "Taylor, I miss you too. I am not sure if I can trust you yet though." Even though this text was far from a proclamation of love, it was my first glimpse of light in what had been a dark couple of months. That word *yet* jumped out of my phone and dangled on my shoulder. I knew this simple word was a symbol of hope, a majestic maybe. I secured the precarious word on my shoulder and tucked it away. I was not going to mess this up. My foot was in the door, and though it was a leviathan door with an unknown force trying to smash my toes, I had a chance. And that is all I cared about.

Over the next few days we started to exchange delicate texts. I was using the word 'sorry' as if it would soon be an unusable and obsolete phrase, as Lilly became friendlier and friendlier while maintaining an understandable and frustrating askance. I prayed I wouldn't say anything off-color, or worse, something that might resurrect the wrong I had done. I texted more carefully and thoughtfully than I ever had before. I felt good about our banter and the direction it was going, but I knew I should not jump into invitations or proposals. The ball was in her court, for I had misused the ball, and defiled the court.

We went two or three days without any communication, and I became extremely restive. I knew that girls had a way of changing their minds with unheard of rapidity. They had the ability to terminate a relationship based off the tiniest notion, or the most trivial happenstance.

A day or two after my anxiety had piqued, I received an unsolicited text from Lilly. "Do you know anything about computers?" It is important to note that I know nothing about computers. I mostly know how to pirate movies, check my e-mail and watch YouTube. But I knew what Lilly was doing. She was giving me an opportunity to come over and "help her with her computer woes," creating a rendezvous without actually admitting that she wanted to see me, as it was too early for that type of surrender. For now she would hold claim to the idea that she simply needed me for my technical expertise. She did this both for my benefit and for hers, believing neither of us was ready to dive back into the waters. In reality I was, but I could not reveal my true needy overzealousness just yet. That ugly beast would make itself known soon enough.

I responded to her putative cry for help, assuring her that I knew everything there was to know about computers. She could probably sense that my computer confidence was overmuch, but she didn't say anything. She had too much grace.

With a final text of capitulation, she asked if I would come over to her new apartment to fix her laptop. I tried to muffle my excitement at her solicitation by simply asking what time she wanted me to come over. We agreed on seven o'clock, enough time for me to buy a new shirt and perfectly coif my hair. I wasn't sure how important this reunion was to her, but it meant everything to me. My life's happiness hung in the balance, and an old T-shirt or rogue hair could easily be my demise. There was no room for error.

I got in my Camry that had almost 300,000 miles on it and drove just over the speed limit to Lilly's new dwelling. I was clad with skinny jeans and a flattering new shirt. I had only the company of my iPod on the ride over, but he comforted me with minstrels of forthcoming victory and felicity. Lilly had moved to an adjacent city, and was now some fifteen minutes away from me. I didn't mind the extra mileage, but it seemed to take forever to arrive at her new address.

I arrived punctually and nervously. She lived by herself in a basement apartment, attached to a residential home; one of those basements that you would never know existed if you were not given specific directions to the descending stairs around back. Her doorstep had four stairs, and barely enough room for the door to fully open. So, I had to knock while standing on the last stair. There she was, mere feet from me, behind a dirty door and a small window.

Lilly swung open the door and greeted me with a hug that was long enough to allow me to smell her hair and instantaneously vow to myself to never take her for granted again, but quick enough to show me she still disapproved of my apparent and recent infidelity.

She dove into small talk, rambling about her new place, her new job and her malfunctioning computer. I walked around in amazement. It was as if I were walking around a vast museum, overtaken by the beauty and intrigue of something I didn't quite understand. She kept on blabbing about this and that, but I could not take my eyes off her. She must have gotten even hotter. I don't understand this transformation that women are able to undertake, but it's something mythical. All the while we were circumventing the very reason, or rather excuse, for my presence, her damaged computer. I hoped it would be something basic she had overlooked, but whatever the problem was it was way over my head. I didn't even know where to start looking. So I fiddled around with it for a few minutes, occasionally mumbling words of exacerbation. Hoping it would not require a departure, I admitted I could not find the problem. "It must be something internal" I opined. Lilly could not have cared less. "Ah well, you wanna watch TV or something?" This was the sexiest thing I had ever heard. Not because of any bawdry language or suggestive intonation, but because it meant that I was right. She had not invited me over just to help her with her computer. She knew I was not a technology wizard; was I really the only person she could think of to look at her device? I am sure I wasn't. Her guise was beautiful and we both understood its purpose.

She was still not ready to jump into my arms. She offered me a seat on the couch, but strategically placed a throw pillow between us to block any extracurricular touching. She flipped through the channels rapidly and landed on a *Law and Order* episode. We watched the drama, and I wondered how I could get rid of the obtrusive pillow that was between me and my girl. But there was much more between us. There were layers of distrust, and complex levels of contradicting feelings. She wanted to be with me, or she wouldn't have invited me over. But she was terrified I would hurt her again. I didn't blame her, but this time it was different. I would have done anything to be her boyfriend now. It's ironic how a few months of skirt-chasing antics will make you crave monogamy.

The show proceeded and the distance remained. Lilly finally mentioned that the couch was very small for two people to comfortably sit and watch TV on. I suggested we move to the floor where we could sprawl out. I also hoped the pillow that acted as a physical mediator between us would be left behind. The pillow joined us. I jokingly commented on the obvious attempt to stop us from cuddling. She laughed and said the buffer was necessary, for she still did not fully trust me.

I have always heard of people talking about sexual tension, and the palpability of it. I had never really understood this before. However, at this moment, pillow between us, legs touching, I could feel it. It was like a volcano was near us, and it was smoking incessantly. Our legs started to entangle themselves and my arm went around her shoulder. The pernicious pillow still remained, but it only blocked our midriffs, and would soon be tossed aside. The smoke from the volcano intensified and thickened. We both feared the eruption, but knew it was only a matter of time before we had molten lava disseminated throughout the living room.

Lilly spoke coyly, "I'm getting tired, why don't you get the lights." I was not that callow; I knew this was another hint. She wanted it. She was just not going to tell me outright. I hopped up and turned off the lights, increasing the comfort and ease of the room. As I returned to her side, the pillow had disappeared and it was replaced by my closeness. The TV had been turned off in my brief absence and a violent calm overtook the room. Something was about to happen.

She turned around and asked if I could massage her neck. You never know if a girl is actually sore, but only a naïf would ask if they were, or how they might have come upon such soreness. You don't ask. You massage. And you do so with intense and sensual gentleness.

A neck massage quickly escalated into a massage of her back and legs. She was lying face down while I straddled her lithe body. I was inebriated by her scent. Her pheromones were raging and bouncing off of me like lottery balls. The last few months of my life had been topsy-turvy at best, and now in that tiny basement alone with Lilly, I felt a sense of completeness. We hadn't talked much, but words were superfluous. We knew what the other was thinking.

The room was now enveloped in a thick dark smoke. An eruption was inevitable, and now we were ready. I flipped over her pliant body and looked at her. Her eyes spoke an unknown language to me. I didn't understand the specifics, but I knew she wanted to be kissed. I touched her face. Her skin was warm and emollient. I inched closer, our noses greeted, and I attacked her lips with months of bent up passion. I had never tasted anything so lovely in all my days. Her lips grabbed mine and held on tightly. Our bodies contorted and the smoke cleared. The volcano had erupted, but it had left a strange tranquility in its wake. All made sense now.

With one kiss everything had returned. My feelings of reluctance and doubt fled and my questionable feelings of love and regret returned tenfold. I could not quite grapple with all that I was feeling, for I was lost in a moment, lost in Lilly's kiss. And in this instance, there was nothing better than being lost.

I am pretty sure that no one had kissed this well in the history of kissing, be it French or any other nationality. We were two people with a rocky past and a precarious future, but our libidos knew nothing of betrayal or dubious forthcomings. So, we continued this quasi-violent barrage of snogging, dismissing anything else that dared to approach our minds. It is hard to think about the future when someone is kissing your neck and grabbing your thighs. You might try, but your focus will be invaded and destroyed. We lay on that thin carpet and kissed for hours. We would stop intermittently to look into each other's eyes and remind ourselves how much we missed each other. It was something out of a young adult novel. It was lunatic love. Of course any utterance of that word would have sent fatal shockwaves through the core of our relationship.

I admit that I was nearing the threshold. I was smitten by this girl that mere months ago had been a tertiary concern of mine. It is truly amazing and disturbing how quickly you can go from simply enjoying somebody's presence to being clumsily and irreparably in love. The word love still frightened me, so let's just agree that I was in the arena.

When we both emerged from our euphoric entwinement we were exhausted. Everybody works up a considerable sweat while kissing; all things considered it's a rather wet activity. But when there is complicated passion involved, it completely sucks you dry. We were now left to face reality. What would Lilly do with me? Would she dismiss this night as an ill-advised moment of weakness? Would she succumb to my cajoling words of repentance? Would I be thrown out in the cold and cutting wind again? These questions terrified me.

We returned to a state of semi-sanity, bereft of panting and closed eyes. I continued to hold her in my arms as we spoke. She kept returning to the topic of distrust. I assured her with every ounce of persuasion and honesty I possessed that I had made an abominable mistake, and I would never make it again. But isn't that what everyone that messes up says? We blame our stupidity and our foggy minds and ask for a second chance. I was realizing that I was no better than the millions of schmucks out there that had knowingly wronged the women in their lives, but still didn't want to let them go. I couldn't let Lilly go, not again.

I had to somehow convince her that I was different from the countless idiot morons of the earth that had nothing but weak excuses and poor behavior to their names, and that frankly were staining the good name of men everywhere.

So I told her that I was sorry, and I would do anything to prove to her that I meant it. She, a little too quickly, came up with an idea. "Ok, I don't think we should kiss for a while then, not until I can trust you again."

I thought this was the worst idea I had ever heard, on par with Marxism and Spam. But sometimes you have to pick some form of political philosophy to avoid anarchy, and you have to consume whatever victuals are left in your kitchen so you do not starve. So, I acquiesced to her capricious plan. What we failed to do was iron out any details to the plan, so for the next few weeks we foundered about in gray areas. Kissing was disallowed, but that apparently only referred to the lips. Any form of light necking, snuggling, cuddling, spooning, excessive hugging, this was all permissible, and made us both want to kiss the other even more. Her wild plan was working, and I even decided not to spend time with any other girls. I wanted to regain her trust, and this time I was not going to fail.

To add to the growing list of hiccups, Lilly had another boy. He had not been in the picture for a long time, but talk of his return had resurfaced since my acts of deviance. He had been doing missionary work on the other side of the world, a two year stint.

Lilly originally told me about this boy at the time we first met. When she first told me about this young man, I had told her I did not want to compete with an old boyfriend. But when I had brought up my distaste for being number two, Lilly had assured me that she would write off Mr. Missionary if I was willing to commit, an answer that sufficed at the time.

Thus, Mr. Missionary remained a non-issue until after I had been banished from Lilly's life. My follies caused her to revert back to what she knew, her past. Now it was time for this young man to return; he would be home in less than a month. I knew very little about him, but I despised him from the onset. Guys have a silly tendency to assume any other man that would have the gall to go out with their girl, be it past, present, or future, is a complete tool and unwavering lowlife. I was no different. I spent too much time thinking about this dude, how unhandsome he was, how much he differed from me and how obviously callow he was. He was twenty-one, and I was twenty-three. Two years is a long time when you are in your twenties and approaching what you consider, often erroneously to be your "best years."

I tried to channel my dislike of Lilly's ex into my efforts of winning her back. I complied with her wishes and did not try to kiss her. I sent thoughtful and probably overly mushy texts. I was gallant to no end, and actually thought I was getting somewhere. Our face time increased week after week. Initially I was lucky to see her two or three times a week, but we started to get to the point where a day without seeing each other was irregular, and two days in a row was just plain abhorrent.

One day we were lying in her bed, refraining from shenanigans, when Lilly confessed something rather unsettling to me. It was unsettling because she didn't have to reveal this to me, especially not at this time. It was like she had to remind me from time to time that I had a poor track record. It was unfair of her. I was on my best behavior and trying to be a better man, but she kept a symbolic pack of salt in her purse that she would sprinkle on my wounds from time to time, wounds that were trying desperately to heal. Lying there inches from her face, Lilly told me that she had, months earlier in an emotional fit, ripped out every extant page of her journal that had mentioned my name. She of course went on this tirade immediately following our second break-up. What was I supposed to say here? Should I have apologized again? Because I am pretty sure my apologies were already becoming redundant and exaggerated. Women have an uncanny ability to make statements or rhetorical questions where no conceivable response in the universe is correct, or even near correct. So I was stuck responding with the classically surly retort of "well, ya..." I had nothing.

A routine began to form between me and my quasi-girlfriend. We would both work during the day, exchange coquettish texts in the afternoon and find our way back to her boudoir at night. There we would watch movies, discuss education reform, kiss each other on the cheek and listen to music; anything save it be kissing on the mouth. That forbidden fruit was killing me. It wasn't that I was so randy I could not contain myself; it is just difficult to be with the one you care most about, knowing how powerful their kiss is, without being able to partake. It's like some carnivorous creature being forced into eating herbs and berries in a jungle full of beasts.

One night it became too much. I was kissing Lilly's cheeks and even grazing the outer corner of her lower lip with my lips. I was playing close to a mouse trap, masochistically hoping I would get snapped. I could handle the abrasion, if it meant I got cheese. As I got closer and closer to the golden ticket that was her mouth, she stopped me. "Why do you have to kiss me?" she asked. "Well, it's not that I have to. It's just hard to be with you and not kiss you." Apparently this was the wrong answer. "So that's all you care about, kissing me? All you care about is my body, is that what this is?" Lilly had her wall up and was interested in battles. Every word that exited my mouth, no matter how careful it was, had the potential of being extremely incriminating. It was as if I, being the culprit, was sleeping with the prosecuting lawyer. I once again pleaded my case, telling Lilly that it was not about lust, it was not about carnal satisfying, it was about her. It was about intimacy and deep feelings. She was not impressed, so I continued. "Lilly I will not kiss or hug you for as long as you want if it means I have a chance to be with you. I will live a life of celibacy with you if that is what you want." Of course I could not remain virginal forever, and would never stand for such extreme cases of chastity, but I had to be very careful with the words I used.

A reluctant smile emerged on her smooth face letting me know my rebuttal was satisfactory. That night I slept over, and we fell asleep like two old metal spoons that had remained unused for years in the same drawer. As always, I woke up trying to hide the giddiness that was splashed over me from waking up next to such an immaculate being. She went to work, and I got in my car and drove home, hoping my morning breath had not sifted into the nostrils of my almost lover. Trying to conceal morning breath from your bedmate is like trying to secretly bake a cake for someone while they are doing the dishes right next to you.

As we spent more and more time together and Mr. Missionary's return neared, things oscillated violently. One day Lilly would appear to be enamored with me like I had arrived at her doorstep on a large white stallion. Other days she would transmogrify into a girl I didn't know, an irritable and moody version of herself that I didn't think existed. She became outrageously unpredictable, and I found that reading her moods became an abstruse practice that was not enjoyable. Still, the good moments outweighed the strange and hard to understand moments.

Lilly was amazing, and I was in love, or at least trying to be. I wouldn't let myself say it; I felt like I had to take a long and complex series of exams to prove I was in love. It couldn't just be said without license or authority of any sort. But there I was, in the dark, searching for love manuals that would help me pass this test that I had failed so many times before.

One unsuspecting Wednesday while Lilly and I were talking and laughing she stopped abruptly, as was her custom, and told me that her ex would be home in less than a fortnight. My body tightened up and I listened closely to her next words like an immigrant with broken English listening to a fast-talking salesman. "I think we should take some time off until he gets back. I can't make any sort of decision about him and our future if you are around consuming my time and thoughts." The tightness of my body recoiled and I was seized with jealous rage. How could she do this to me? And how could she want this jerk over me? Again I felt I was in no position for bargaining, so I bit my tongue and lied. "I understand. That makes perfect sense." Lilly clearly had thought this through and was not going to be persuaded otherwise.

Lilly made it clear that she was not sure she was going to get back with the dreaded ex, but rather that he deserved a chance. I personally thought he deserved nothing more than a courtesy text telling him that a new man was in town, named Taylor. But as we know, I was not calling the shots.

The following two weeks felt like a long summer at your grandma's. I was given rather stringent instructions to not call or text Lilly during the boyfriend interim; apparently she would contact me when her inner conflict had been cozily resolved. So I went about my quotidian endeavors, hanging out with my friends, eating cheap pizza and abstaining from women. I had found for the third time that life without Lilly was not especially rosy. I certainly didn't verbalize this to anyone, but I yearned for her. I lay in bed at night thinking about her hands, her voice, and the music of our conversations. I was lucky to live with three of my best friends, so I was not a complete wreck. I hadn't even told them about the forced hiatus I was in. They had witnessed my first break down; I figured I would save any further humiliation for later, in case I lost Lilly again. That idea was unthinkable, but at the same time it was a very real actuality that gave me the shivers.

Lilly taught at a ritzy and newly constructed elementary school about thirty minutes away, next to houses that looked more like medieval fortresses. I knew that parent-teacher conference was in a couple of days. I also knew that this stressed her out beyond belief. A few unruly students and a litany of overprotective workaholic parents made for thick air and a stressful environment. Her ex-boyfriend that would soon return after a two year absence could only add to her levels of discomfort and uneasiness. And on top of all that, she had a Taylor somewhere in the mix of things. Whatever that meant.

I knew Lilly's week was going to be emotional, and that moist remnants of mascara would defile her pillows. I wanted to do something, but I knew a hand-on-the-shoulder text would not suffice. I vacillated over the degree of romance. There is a fine line between a suave display of affection and an overzealous act of romantic bravado. I figured, like millions of men have, that flowers would do the trick. I wouldn't send roses. Roses spelled anniversaries and overwhelming love. I would send a mixture, something aesthetically pleasing, something a florist would admire, something less red.

I drove to the Flower Patch, heeded my own advice and purchased a blend of flowers that was pretty, but not stunning. The florist seemed pleased with my decision and embarrassingly aware of the fact that I had never set foot in a flower shop, let alone sent a floral arrangement to a woman of interest. The flower men informed me that they required an address and a time of delivery. This was easy. My plan was to send the flowers to her at school, so she would be thoroughly surprised. I also knew that her students and co-workers would ask her who the mysterious lothario was. I knew that Mr. Missionary was not going to be sending gifts of any sort, so if nothing else my stock would rise, while his lay dormant and gathered moss.

I finished my amorous note and attached it to the vase, finalizing the transaction. They would deliver my delicate plants to Lilly's workplace the next day right after lunch. I had no idea what to expect. I added in my message that I did not require any response or reciprocation. I just wanted her to know I was thinking about her, and wanted her to feel better. I was unfamiliar with floral exchange and the appropriate protocol. Maybe I was not even supposed to be sending anything that could blossom to a girl who was on the fence about me. I was in over my head, but that's how I lived and perhaps where I was most comfortable.

The next day I waited. I knew Lilly would receive her multicolored arrangement between one and two o'clock in the afternoon. I wanted a text within about ten seconds of the delivery, but I knew I likely wouldn't hear from her until her school day was over. I checked my phone every two or three minutes hoping for something warm and affirming, but saw nothing. It was nearing five o'clock and I was panicking. What if she found my gesture off-putting and uncouth? What if the pedestrian flower men had botched the delivery? What if she thought nothing of them at all? Was that possible? My head was riddled with worry and unreasonable scenarios.

Twenty minutes later I still hadn't heard from her. I gave up like you do when your opponent has littered the Monopoly board with hotels. The game isn't over necessarily, but you have likely thrown in the towel. I was probably premature in giving up, but it was easier to do that than hopelessly wait, and then be crushed by silence.

I was adjusting the AM/FM transmitter when I felt my phone vibrate. It was an extended vibration, signaling to me that it was not just a text but a phone call. A million things rushed in and out of my brain before I had a chance to look at the screen to identify the caller. With hopeful glee I glanced down in my lap and saw the caller I.D. ----Lilly!

"Hello?" I answered coyly.

"Taylor…"

"Hey, what's going on? How was work?"

Her voice cracked ever so slightly, but I caught it.

"Tay, I can't believe you did that."

"Did what?" I asked, knowing that she had received the flowers and was overjoyed with the gesture.

"The flowers Tay, that was seriously so thoughtful. I was having a terrible week, and I don't know how you knew that. You are like the sweetest guy I have ever met."

The second she said that, I wanted to press pause on our phone call, and record that last sentence with numerous and expensive recording devices. People have a tendency to forget the things they say, especially when emotion is present. And I needed her to remember that I was the sweetest guy she had ever met, because that meant that I was sweeter than her ex ever was or ever could be. Her words, not mine. Alas, the technology for such chicanery was not available, so I just hoped she would remember, and I hoped desperately that she meant it.

We talked for a few minutes and her voice told me that she was sincere. Lilly may have been recently plagued with moodiness and frequent episodes of crying, but one thing she could not do was mask her sincerity. Some people can effortlessly alter their levels of enthusiasm and voice intonations to coincide with a moment, and others are incapable of the smallest fib. Lilly was of the latter disposition.

We hung up and I was filled with a happiness that I prayed would remain. Only insecure people are unhappy when they are happy, because they know felicity is a fleeting thing. This bothered me, because I was usually a beacon of optimism. I knew that happiness didn't always last, but when I was happy I was happy. But for the moment my happiness was overshadowed by fear. I feared that this was one of the last moments I would feel happy by the hands of Lilly.

I can't really explain it, but some feelings that arrive in your gut are accompanied by an unknown, unspoken, and ominous guarantee. Just like retail guarantees, they aren't 100%, but they are correct enough to make you dizzy with worry. People talk about knowing they are going to die soon, or knowing the second they lay eyes on someone, that they will be their spouse. It is a strange phenomenon, but I believe in it. Every once and a while my clairvoyant predictions are wrong, but I felt so strongly that this would be one of the last good moments with Lilly, and that left me sad and spooked. I prayed that I was reading things wrong, and that we would have countless memories of bliss and delight in our future.

I knew exactly the day that Lilly's Missionary was going to return. I knew the hour, and part of me thought she would call me from the airport telling me that she found her returned man to be repulsive and unbecoming, nothing in comparison to me. But I received no such call.

The day came and went, and I heard nothing. This was the texting episode all over again, except this was days not hours of torture. Three days passed and I still hadn't heard from her. Six days had passed and the silence was breaking my heart. I felt like I couldn't be the first to text her. What kind of weak and needy man would that make me? So I resisted. I wasn't in the best emotional shape, but I wasn't going to be that guy.

Then I texted her. It was ill-advised, but I was being eaten inside by the lack of communication. At this point I would have felt better if she had just told me to go to a certain underworld known for its high temperatures. I just had to hear something. Even though it's unsettling, when we hear thunder at least we know the storm is coming.

I took out my phone with shaky confidence and texted Lilly, saying "Hey, I know I shouldn't be texting you, but I have to know what's going on. Are you dating him? Are we done? Just give me something." I'm sure she read that text and started dry-heaving from the desperation, but I was passed caring. It was crunch time, and I had to pull out all the stops.

Heaven forbid she read the text and respond quickly. It was as if she knew I was suffering between each electronic exchange of words. So to remain in pattern, Lilly waited a solid five hours before responding with a terse "Hey Tay, sorry I haven't texted you. Things are kind of crazy right now. And I'm not sure what is going to happen." This was a supremely abysmal response. It gave me almost no helpful information. All it did was tell me she remained in the gray and nebulous middle that benefited no one. She wasn't posting pictures with her returned man on social media outlets, so I had no form of inconspicuous espionage.

Over the next couple of weeks my heart seemed to sink slowly downward into my chest like a barefoot does upon making its first step into thick mud. I knew things were ending and that Lilly just did not have the heart to tell me, especially until things had become more serious with that amateur lover of hers.

I had lost all pride and would text Lilly from time to time to retrieve painful updates about her relationship status. Her responses were always covered in brevity and stinging ambiguity. She knew what she was doing. She was trying to secure what had once made her happy and had never betrayed her, while trying to hold in possible reserve the dashing new love that proved perilous and untrustworthy. It was excruciatingly ironic to watch this game be played, since I had on sundry occasions been on the other side of the table, the one juggling two callers. Love is never perfect, we all know this, but even in its finest and purest form it is fatal, and will often destroy those involved. I wasn't destroyed yet, but I could hear the distant cracking of thunder and was almost certain a tsunami was brewing somewhere in the nearby sea.

Lilly's texts became more and more worthless. They reeked of indifference, which hurt me more than hate could. I hadn't thrown in the towel completely, but I had the towel in my hand so I could throw it at a moment's notice.

As the weeks piled up, I retreated back into my mediocre life. My studies had teamed up with my heart and had decided to suffer side by side. I was failing more than one class and had little interest in amending my shortcomings. When your head is barely above water you don't concern yourself with your swimming technique, you just try not to swallow water. And so was my present life; I had no interest in improving myself and progressing, I just wanted to stay alive. I just wanted to not be depressed.

I started meeting new girls, with the hope of forgetting Lilly, but I could do no such thing. Meeting them, even flirting with them came easy as it always had, but I could not propel it any further than that. My apathy towards the opposite sex made it impossible for me to think about anyone but Lilly, the one who had left me useless and unimportant.

For whatever reason, it seems that some of the greatest and most rough and tumble conversations I have ever had on the telephone have occurred while in my car. This is a good thing since I am usually unencumbered by company or distractions. This next phone call was no different, it was momentous and unexpected. Lilly had called me on my way home from school. She wanted to meet for dinner. What in the name of Zeus could this mean? I was so unbelievably exhausted from the last couple months of teeter-tottering. I was ready to commit or bow out. We agreed to meet at the Italian Place, a sandwich shop famous for its succulent Philly cheese steaks.

I arrived first and waited nervously in my car, unable to hear the words reverberating from the radio speakers. I saw her pull up in her beat-up silver Honda Accord. Man she was beautiful. I hadn't seen in her in over a month. My body ached to touch hers, and to scream out feelings that I had shoved deep into my soul, and of course to kiss her. I had to kiss her again.

She got out of her car, clad in tight blue jeans and a dark blouse whose design was obscured by her breathtaking figure. She flashed a real smile at me that explained how glad she was to see me. Something had happened. I could feel it. Mr. Missionary had to have screwed up, there had to be some misdeed or foul play on his part. We hugged quickly and entered the restaurant where loud TV's echoed various sporting events. In the background men ate enormous sandwiches covered in pepper on uncomfortable black metal chairs. Lilly ordered, and I picked up the tab. She was clearly famished from the battle between her heart and mind. Or maybe it was because women forget to eat meals when they are busy and stressed. At any rate she devoured her Philly while I wondered what sort of conversation was going to transpire after we were well satiated.

Nothing remained of our meal but crust and silence when Lilly spoke. She dove head first into her explanation of what had been a hellish couple of weeks. She explained that she felt obligated to her ex, because of their history. She felt she had to give him a chance, and that would be impossible if she was talking to me at all. As she described the confusion that characterized her recycled relationship, I chimed in with simple questions. But I did not really care. All I wanted to know was that she was done with him, and ready for me. I skimmed through the words she spoke, listening for some glimmer of hope, a silver lining indicator of my future happiness. I didn't find anything especially salient, but I listened on. She proceeded to tell me some interesting things about Mr. Missionary. Apparently he was terribly unaffectionate and she was suspicious of his sexual preference. He had been a ballroom dancer before his missionary service, which for all intents and purposes is a red flag of homosexuality. Normally I do not concur with the hateful stereotypes or pejorative language concerning the gays, but when a sexually confused man is the adjacent line segment in my twisted love triangle, for better or worse, my inner homophobe emerges.

As our weird conversation continued, Lilly's hand made its way across the table and was intercepted effortlessly by mine. Our fingers interconnected perfectly without the slightest fumble like two parts of a clock that know no other function. I saw a pain in her eyes that somehow jumped across the table and met me square on. I no longer cared about her light-footed counterpart, I cared about her. I listened more intently as our legs started accosting one another. Something was happening. She was coming back.

We talked for two hours, and left only because the employees were mopping around us, hinting at our departure. Our conversation moved to my car, where Lilly quickly coiled her body up and put her arms around me across the seat. This is what it was all about. I could have remained there, speechless in my car for days. It is difficult to realize the magnitude of moments until they are long gone, but this one I could recognize its ineffable importance.

We didn't come to any sort of conclusion, but it was a step in the right direction. Lilly promised she would communicate better with me, and I believed her. I patiently waited for her correspondence over the next few days, imbued with a new sense of hope. I still did not know what would come of this triangle, but my imagination was impervious to the what-ifs. I had visions of tuxedos and white dresses, children and family photos. My thoughts leaped over time zones and boundaries, landing in unhealthily optimistic pastures.

A few days later it was decided that a date between Lilly and me would be appropriate. We met at a hole-in-the-wall Mexican restaurant where the parking lot was lined in gravel and the employees barely spoke English. Lilly was always fun to eat out with. Even though she was in many ways the quintessential damsel, a little prissy and always dressed to the nines, she could eat with the best of them. Somehow her princess frame could withstand massive portions of greasy and sludgy food. This was a turn-on.

We sat down and began the back and forth that goes hand-in-hand with dining. Our table was so big that a fraction of our intimacy had been removed. We were forced to raise our decibels slightly in order to hear each other and to hold or touch hands would require an exaggerated effort. The food was scrumptious and reminded me of the many nights we had shared in run-down restaurants eating cheesy treats. Lilly was a gift. I simply had not understood her value, like a kid that dismisses a vintage action figure as a kitsch toy and fails to realize the incredible value it contains. This was Lilly. At first she was lovely, fun and somewhat disposable. But with time I learned that she was worth more than the U.S. Mint could ever produce.

At the end of the meal a swarthy server in his thirties asked me in Spanish if the lady across from me was my girlfriend. Lilly did not know Spanish, but the question still paralyzed me. Whenever you are speaking a foreign tongue around other people a small part of you wonders if somehow those present picked up the gist of your conversation. It is nerve-rattling. I responded with a trite "Well no, but it's complicated." I fretted that she would catch that last word, *complicado*, it wouldn't take a linguist to discern what that meant. But I really had no reason to stress. Things were complicated, and Lilly knew that much.

I paid for the dinner that would prove to be the last time I would ever eat with Lilly. We exited the restaurant that appeared to be made mostly of aluminum and shuffled around in the parking lot for a few minutes before we said goodbye. Kissing was still taboo, or at least something I was not going to initiate, so hugs were my only prize. Despite eating to near capacity, I felt empty. Lilly had a disturbing way of making me feel whole and despicably empty all within the space of an hour.

The next couple weeks of my life were confusing to say the least. For a brief and fleeting moment I thought I had won Lilly back. Our dinners and touching had toyed with my stupid heart. Lilly became terribly elusive. She responded to my texts, but only with one or two word responses. We would see each other every once and a while, but something fundamental was missing. I was still walking on a paper-thin sheet of porcelain so I refrained from calling out Lilly for her difficultness.

I did not see her for seven or eight days when we finally met up again. She was apparently strapped for time, which women tend to be when their interest is waning. So we went for a quick drive. I needed to talk to her. We parked in a church parking lot and I got down to business. I told her that I had not kissed another girl since our fallout, and that I was willing to do anything, anything to be with her. She listened, but her eyes were darting all over the place, like a truly unsure person. She recanted with the tired excuse that she still did not trust me fully, and was simply not sure what would happen with us. I became frustrated and drove her back to her car. I had no idea that this would be the last time I would be in such close proximity to the girl that made my body and soul cringe and grin simultaneously. We hadn't gotten in a big fight or anything, simply a discussion that wasn't going anywhere, so we both agreed to retire for the night.

The next day I texted Lilly, first thing in the morning. Nothing. The following day I remained silent, now flowing with selfish pride. If she wanted to see me, she would make it happen. That attitude lasted another three or four days. I texted her again, this time with new adjectives and clever attempts at humor. Nothing. After all we had been through, was she really ending things by ignoring me? I felt sick. My thoughts turned into a rotten soup, thick and distasteful. I had screwed up, but I didn't deserve this deep freeze.

I accepted another week of silence and unreturned correspondence, and then I lost it. I signed on to Facebook and started composing the letter of my life. The tone of my cyber missive jutted back and forth and mercilessly weaved in and out like a frosty fjord. I started out with a juvenile 'How could you/who do you think you are?' voice, and then returned to my old friend, the apology. After profusely typing words of repentance I told her in not a few words what made her so special to me, and why I couldn't let go. I always fancied myself as somewhat of a wordsmith, but this was my finest work. This message had the epistolary weight of Victorian majesty. I even used a few words I knew Lilly would not know, to remind her of my omniscient intellect. The letter was gorgeous and was sent.

Within the hour I received a message in return. This was the ultimate moment. I saw the red on top of the page that indicated I had an unread message. I opened it and saw that it was not lacking in content. Whatever Lilly had to say she had thought about it. This meant one of two things: She wanted me back, or it was over. I felt like someone had pushed a heavy box of tools on my chest before I even started reading. My eyes saw the words and read quickly to get to the highlights. I knew she would not pepper her message with drabble, so I cruised through searching for her verdict. Lilly folded to the clichéd ways of ending things with the written word. She started by telling me what a splendid gentleman I was, followed by touching on a few specific qualities of mine that were appealing to her (just not appealing enough). I had now read 70% of her message without hearing the final verdict, but I knew it was over. I could hear her voice; I could see her avoiding eye contact with me and decidedly writing me off forever.

The final paragraph was a fatal bullet. No matter how ready you are for death, for the end, it is still a jolt. It still hurts in new ways and makes you wish you were anywhere else in the world experiencing anything else. It's euphoric, yet clear and debilitating.

"Tay I wanted to apologize for not communicating very well this past couple of weeks. I met somebody and we have started dating. I'm sorry." After hitting me with a cannonball in the gut, she asked if I wanted my books back that I had loaned her. This is like informing someone that they are fired, but that they can take home three, maybe even four stacks of sticky-notes.

I was furious. I felt like hurling insults that only street thugs would understand. Who on earth was this guy? I thought I was in a love triangle, not some demented square. This whole time Lilly was supposed to be conflicted between new scary love and erstwhile love, not brand new infatuation. She was supposed to be writing songs about her inner battle, not out meeting jaunty men in leather jackets. I was outraged and obliterated. I responded with a blithe "Keep the books, have a good life, adieu."

I was absolutely verklempt. I cried alone in my room hoping that none of my roommates were around. What hurt so bad was that I didn't even know who this guy was. I didn't know if Lilly had been slithering around behind my back or if some dashing prize-fighter of a man had fallen in her lap and promised her the world. I had no information to help ease my depression, not even Facebook photos.

Ch. 5- Residual Effects

"Moving on is easy. It's staying moved on that's trickier." ~

Katerina Stoykova Klemer

This is the point where things got weird. They had been depressing for a while, but now the beast of depression had grown another head and attacked me like an underfed demon. I am not sure what to call this Siamese brother of Depression, but I know he is evil and wants to drag me through the rocks.

Lilly and I were through. I had to deal with that fact, and for some time I dealt with it in what I considered a relatively healthy manner. I deleted her from my phone, deleted her from my Facebook and stopped all communication with her. Unlike Slikowski, Lilly was determined to remain estranged from me post-breakup. She no longer sent me texts of her feelings that dangled hazardously in the air. She no longer liked my photos on Facebook, and no longer appeared to be in existence at all.

I may have deleted Lilly from Facebook, but I did not block her. This was a highly strategic move. It enabled me to surreptitiously cyber stalk anyone foolish or vain enough to not have their Facebook page on private. Lilly's page was not on private. I could peruse her pictures as I felt it was necessary. I would not be bombarded by her posts or updates, but when my curiosity climaxed, I would not meet a dead end.

I remained strong in the following weeks. I thought about Lilly, but her final message to me was clear and unwavering. She did not want to be with me anymore. I would never know for certain if it was because of my shortcomings, or because of this mystery man that had moon- walked into her life. That stuck with me like a petulant itch in an unreachable spot. I would never know the ultimate catalyst, the blade that tore us apart.

I didn't look at her pictures for a long time. I tried to move on and forget her. This effort was aided by a slew of young women and questionable decisions. I was forming quite the untoward pattern of behavior: Date girl, break up with girl, mourn over girl, and indulge myself with large amounts of fine women. My intentions weren't all that bad. I figured the more girls I went out with the greater my odds would be of finding the right one. I had met both Slikowski and Lilly in the course of one of my lustful rampages. So my irresponsible behavior couldn't be all that bad.

I returned to some old lovers and rejoined the unofficial club of happy people. Life was easy and exciting. I lived with my best friends in the world. I worked long and hard in the summer so I was not penniless during the rest of the year, and could focus on school and my full-time job of finding a mate. My nights were filled with playing basketball in churches and hot- tubbing with like-minded millenials. Almost every single day I ate out for lunch and dinner, and three or four of those days dinner would be for two. Despite what I sometimes thought, I was young and nearing the prime of my life. I was twenty-four and was finally starting to understand things that had never even entered my thoughts when I was twenty-one.

Sometimes when we are happy, or at least content with life, we feel like tossing the dice. I'm not sure if it is delusions of invincibility, or if we are simply bored with the status quo, but we are at times constrained to mix things up, to poison the well of good fortune.

When I started looking at Lilly's Facebook page it did not spiral me down into depression or elicit ugly acts of vengeance, but it certainly shook my state. I would open up albums on my computer and see this new guy. He was good looking, muscular with annoyingly white teeth. His smile looked like it was manufactured in a dank factory in China. His tight fitting shirts bothered me. But most of all I was bothered at how Lilly looked at him. It was a look I had been on the receiving end of before, and I had taken it for granted. There are some things between man and woman that surpass the greatness of physical touch. When two sets of eyes catch a hold of each other and hold on, it is beautiful and poetic. No amount of petting can compete with this feature of love, and there it was, mocking me on my own dusty computer screen.

How did Lilly already have so many pictures with this bruiser? She just met him. I'm not sure why some people find the need to flaunt their debutante relationships. It must bolster them up to some nifty plateau of self-righteous majesty that makes them cooler than everyone else. Or maybe I was just bitter. But I think I was right about this one.

At least they weren't engaged. I could not handle that after mere weeks of grieving. These were just declaration photos; declarations of young love and worriless lives. I was okay with this.

I didn't think they would break up, but there was still a chance. Relationships are never certain, especially if a ring is nowhere to be seen.

Then out of nowhere it was seen. A ring emerged. It was a few weeks after my initial phase of back-sliding. I moseyed back onto the internet to check on the status of Lilly and this dude who just looked pedantic. To my unnerving chagrin, I saw that the two were now engaged. A giant diamond was on the screen looking at me. Although I looked at every solitary photograph that was posted, it was all a blur. All I saw were flowers, a bended knee, and a shattered dream.

In a way it was good, maybe now I could move on at last. Hope was destroyed, but it left me room to walk forward when I had been standing still or treading backward for so long. Before the tears could be produced in their ducts I exited out of the page, threw my laptop on my bed and left the room. I had to go shoot around. Basketball was the only answer. I put in headphones and shot around for hours, as I had done before and would do again following any sort of heartache. I wasn't one to consume alcohol, so in order to get my mind off something I had to get my endorphins pumping; and whether that involved a basketball hoop, or a thin 18-year old co-ed, I never woke up hugging a toilet, wincing from a lingering headache.

Many engagement rings are returned to stores, and many hearts never recover from a ruptured promise to wed. But the reality is most proposals that are accepted snowball into the inevitable party of vows and ecclesiastical endorsement: a wedding. I told myself on more than one occasion that such a relationship appearing as abruptly and mysteriously as a tornado was doomed to have the same consequences of a tornado, destruction and nothingness. Alas, my selfish thoughts were wrong, like they had been so many times before. Lilly and this guy, whose name I never bothered to remember, married. They were happy, and this irked me to no end. To no surprise, I was not invited to their celebration. I under no circumstances would have attended, but a courtesy invite would have been appreciated. Truth be told, I would have foamed at the mouth with jealous rage had I received a gaudy invite to their unholy matrimony. So, I was sad and inordinately pissed for a few days. Okay, maybe a few weeks. But the beautiful part about an ex-lover getting married is that you truly have no choice but to forget them and move on. Right? You cannot pine over some other person's legalized and solemnized property can you? Well, I suppose you can, but it is much more repugnant and frowned upon.

About a month later the foggy veneer of confusion and regret started to dissipate from my mind. Lilly was gone, and it was mostly my fault. I could live with it. It's not like we dated and were in love for years. It was a casual affair, without the casualness and with more maddening ups and downs. But it was over, and I could be a big boy now. Despite his poor grammar, Bob Marley was right on point when he mused, "No woman, no cry."

I started to enjoy my life more than I had in the last few months. When you are desperately chasing a woman, you only focus on the blissful moments of ecstasy. But after the fact you remember how miserable the chase was, how most of your nights ended in solitude and frustration. To help myself heal I began reviewing Lilly's flaws in my mind, in a feeble attempt to feel better about her absence. This worked for a little bit. How could I be with someone that constantly wore bejeweled jeans and had eyeliner tattooed to their eyelids? How could I respect myself, being with someone who knew nothing about sports and listened to the kind of country music that should not be allowed in urban cities? Lilly was great, but her hair wasn't as long as I preferred it, and her lips were not as full as they should be. Perhaps she wasn't the masterpiece I had conjured up in my head. Maybe she was but a fallible, sometimes obtuse girl who had no idea what she really wanted in life. These were all lies, but they helped get me through my struggle.

With my new philosophy and spare time, I started courting new girls. They were all unlike Lilly, and I viewed this as an intake of crisp new air. There was no need to be stifled by my past, so I decided to rid myself of negative thoughts and self-deprecating practices. I made a larger effort to involve myself in my religion and my friendships. I never could manage to have female friends if benefits were not involved, but I was blessed with a rich circle of male chums, and they buoyed me through thick and dangerous waters.

Months piled up like overdue library books forgotten under my bed, and this was good. Lilly barely, if ever crept into my subconscious. I went to New Orleans. I ate alligator meat. I went to New York City for the first time. I was now the head sophomore basketball coach at Provo High School. I didn't need Lilly. Life was great, and I was getting along just fine without her perfect voice and infectious charisma. I didn't need that. I had plenty of options. I was twenty-four and had plenty of tomfoolery ahead of me. I could save love for another era.

I have always been extremely thin. I am 6'3" and 165 lbs. in jeans and army boots. I tried lifting weights in high school, but all it did was keep my coaches off my back. I hadn't lifted any sort of iron in years. I was content with my scrawny frame and had no real desire to consume large portions of protein and other assorted supplements to increase my appeal with the opposite sex. I was athletic and lean, and relied heavily on my superior patter rather than bulging muscles.

My friends did not agree with my skinny-man rationale. They wanted me to join the gym, and lift on a daily basis with them. After lengthy and creative cajoling I finally acquiesced. If nothing else I would use the basketball court, sauna and hot tub if muscles could not be produced.

One afternoon after a hardwood cardio workout I was leaving the gym when I saw something that disturbed me. It wasn't a fat person, and it was not a mirage, despite the heat and oncoming dehydration. It was Lilly. She was twenty yards away from me, conspicuously running on a treadmill. Her hair was different, and her chest looked bigger. She didn't see me, but I saw her. I hadn't seen her in what felt like eons. I wasn't keeping track, but it had been months, many months. She looked amazing, drenched in sweat and completely unaware of my presence. I inched forward with my phone in one hand and my iPod in the other. I pressed pause as to remove the distraction of noise, but I kept the headphones in so any attempt at conversation would be futile. I expected a painfully awkward head nod or forced hello. I tried to just walk out, looking at my feet but my head wouldn't allow it. It stiffened upward and demanded eye contact. I was now ten, maybe fifteen feet from her. Nothing. She was transfixed in her stationary position. I imagined she was running from something, maybe her husband. But I only toyed with the thought momentarily, just enough to send chills down my bony back. I returned to my car in the parking lot and sat in my car for a few minutes. My thoughts were not doing a good job at forming themselves. All I could articulate in my mind was "Damn." But I think that says enough. I couldn't believe how beautiful she still was. When you break up with someone for good, you always secretly hope that they will gain sixty pounds or that their teenage acne will return or perhaps they will lose all their teeth in a horrific dental catastrophe. Unfortunately, this rarely happens. They usually look better. They look well-rested, better dressed and perky in all the right places. This makes us fear that the reason they look so good is because now we are gone. They look better because that diseased monkey is off their back. And that is a tough thought to entertain.

The Lilly encounter at the gym only happened once, and only fazed me for twenty-four hours or so. No major setbacks. The next accidental encounter I had with her was more detrimental, because it was coupled with two other bump-ins all in the space of one week.

Once again I had a month or two of peace. I madeout with a 35-year old single mother of four, and was back to my care-free life. School progressed slowly, and a much needed Christmas break was nigh. During the break my family came to town and per custom we saw nearly every movie that came out. It was our way of celebrating the yuletide. One night I was elected to return to the concessions during previews to purchase popcorn and soda. Just as I paid for the treats and attempted to juggle the buckets of soda and butter-soaked popcorn I saw Lilly out of the corner of my eye. This time she saw me.

"Tay! How are you?" She rushed towards me with arms open. I managed a small smile and hugged back. I worried that my immediate hurt would be visible, and might even carry a certain odor. It seemed to go unnoticed. She gesticulated that her husband was waiting in the theater. We hugged again and said goodbye with at least one of us lying that it was good to see each other. The popcorn was delicious, but seeing Lilly kind of ruined the movie for me.

Three days later, back at the same Cinemark, I ran into Lilly again. This time it was in the parking lot with my family as we were leaving and she was entering, this time with her chic husband in stride. This encounter hardly lasted two seconds. They were in a hurry, and this time a wave and brief smile sufficed. This was the first time I saw *him* in the flesh. I didn't like his face. Its symmetry made me want to vomit. But nothing about him remained with me. What remained were Lilly's lime-green skinny jeans. They fit her better than any pant had ever fit any one person in the history of legs.

As if these two run-ins were not painful enough, the very next day I saw Lilly again. I only saw her next to me in a white car at a stoplight, but three times in a week was more than I had seen her in nearly a year. My mind started racing unhealthily. I wondered if there was a reason for all of this. Were our chance meetings part of some great cosmic design? Was she having marital issues? I wasn't even sure what city she lived in. I just knew we were in the same metropolitan area. Could it really be just blind luck that I saw her thrice in one seven day period?

These were moronic thoughts. The universe was not trying to tell me anything. If anything this was just a reminder from the heavens that I needed to get over Lilly. So once again I tossed and twisted in my bed for four or five days and convinced myself that I did not care about Lilly, and that I was better off.

It took me a couple months to really get over that unfortunate series of encounters. I would go several days at a time without thinking about Lilly, sometimes even a full week. I was regularly dating and kissing my share of women, for I believed in the axiom 'The best way to get over someone, is to get under someone else.' The reoccurring truth, however, was that no matter how many torrid notches I accrued on my belt, I was still left thinking about the one that got away.

I hated that phrase, 'the one that got away.' It was not as if I had a hold of her leg, and she was simply stronger than me. I walked away from her months ago, and now I was on the wrong side of the karmic spectrum lamenting my losses. All in all she didn't 'get away', I pushed her away, and then I felt sorry for myself when she wouldn't come back.

People don't really have new advice when it comes to breakups. You hear time and time again that you 'just need time,' or that 'everything will work out.' These platitudes are usually right, but they don't make anyone feel better. It is like telling someone that just got shot in the arm to quit crying because an arm wound is not fatal. It is true, but not especially helpful or insightful.

Despite my disdain for these "words of comfort," I tried to come to grips with the fact that I did just need time, and that everything would end in happiness and overused clichés.

While I was systematically moving on, Lilly was off conceiving a child. My periodic cyber stalkings of her Facebook page finally revealed to me that she was pregnant. This image of a woman with child did two things to me. First it made me sprint through irrational hypotheticals. Would Lilly and I have gotten pregnant that fast? What would our offspring look like? What would her child look like now? What would she name it? Then I turned a corner and went a different direction. Clearly she had gained weight. Her face looked round and pasty. Her stomach had obviously ballooned up, and her entire body looked like it was reacting poorly to an allergic reaction. My thoughts were terribly unkind, but I justified them since they would never be vocalized.

I'm not sure what I was expecting, but nine months later, to my surprise and discomfort a child was born. This actually gave me some solace. You can't in your right mind be upset at an infant. You cannot look at a new-born and be disgusted at its creation. They were now a family, a unit, an exclusive cadre that I would never be a part of. But who was I to remain bitter at a beautiful new family? Their family pictures were adorable, their love obvious and their tenderness apparent. I was sick of feeling like a jerk. Only a jerk would harbor vile thoughts towards a great person who just happened to move on, who happened to be happier. But was being a jerk not an unavoidable part of my male DNA? Or was acting like a jerk merely an excuse that men had discovered centuries ago to excuse themselves from their perpetually bad behavior? Whatever the cause of my cowardice, I was done.

Two years had passed since Lilly had gotten married. She had had a child and I had had various failed relationships. At this point I was not thinking about her anymore. Her whereabouts became a mystery, and the details of her life became irrelevant. No matter how hard I tried, I could not wish her anything but complete happiness. My only real mistake was keeping all of her amateur song recordings on my iPod. For months the sound of her voice pierced me like an unexpected dart when one of her songs made its way through the Rolodex of my iTunes shuffle mode. Just like I could have blocked her from Facebook, I could have deleted these songs, but I was a nostalgic fellow. I still had grade-school pictures of my 3rd grade girlfriend that had been swapped after picture day. Even if they created microbursts of pain, I enjoyed the physical footnotes of the books that told the stories of my life.

Keeping Lilly's songs on more than one device didn't exactly expedite the healing process, but with time her tracks became not unlike the crinkled old elementary school pictures. They were just fond memories and reminders of a different time. No matter the amount of pain that love and the lack of love can create, there will always remain a few salient moments that will forever be worth the turmoil and seemingly endless angst.

Ch. 6- More Women, More Failures & Less Money

"That would be nice."

Charlie Brown on hearing that in life you win some and lose

some.

~Charles Schulz

I was now in my junior year of college. Most people my age had been graduated for three years, but I did things at my own pace, even if I wasn't particularly fond of my own pace. There was a girl I often saw on campus. She was slender and had long curly blonde hair. She looked like Taylor Swift, but even prettier. Despite their being upwards of 35,000 students at the university, I probably saw this girl once or twice a week. Our schedules managed to coincide at the library or various eating spots. She was so pretty that guys were constantly approaching her. Each one approached her with a clever new pick-up line, usually leaving without her phone number or hand, but still pleased with themselves that they found the courage to talk to her. She wasn't the type of girl that wandered about in large cliques. She was a lone fox, and seemed content to read her textbook and coyly smile at hopeful men.

I never managed to talk to her. She was a mythical creature, not a girl I could casually talk to in hopes of a date. One day I was studying at the library with my friend Bryce when I saw her again. My homework was being interrupted by the constant breaks I took to gawk in her direction. When I had finally gathered enough self-discipline to stop fixating on this beautiful stranger and finish my essay, it was too late. Bryce had pounced. We hadn't even discussed my longing for this majestic being. He just had more *cajones* than me. Bryce and I were both tall, both dark haired and debatably handsome. We were both basketball players and had dated many of the same women. These similarities made us very competitive. We rarely fought, but there were many times when the action of one of us irked the other beyond belief. So, I wasn't mad at Bryce, just mad that he got his wily paws on her first.

Bryce and Miss Apkins went out two or three times. I guess they kissed and rolled around a bit, but Bryce lost interest. I approached him about her a few days after the fact to inquire about her availability. He tossed a caustic comment my way about how crazy she was and how I could "go for it" if I really wanted to.

Let me briefly explain the thought process here of most men. So-called crazy girls really don't faze us. If you ask enough people, almost anyone can be categorized as loony, and besides that, craziness is a very subjective thing. What is absurd and nefarious to one is cute and playful to another. Bryce and I had fairly similar tastes in appearance and personality, so I should have been concerned. So why wasn't I? Because the hotter a girl is, the less I or any other guy for that matter concerns himself with her eccentricities. We convince ourselves that what on the surface seems outlandish and childish is in reality delightful and idiosyncratic. We consider ugly outbursts to be quirky anomalies and fits of rage to be but signs of stress. All the while we are enamored with the way the girl looks, especially next to us, and especially in public. If an unequivocally gorgeous woman throws a tantrum in a department store, guys remember all the people staring at them, especially the envious men. They almost dismiss the godawful display, remembering only the jealousy of the male onlookers. It is a terrible flaw we have, but it happens all the time. I would soon find out how this rule applied to me.

I messaged Apkins on Facebook. She knew I was friends with Bryce, but she still agreed to go out with me. But first she asked me, what to her was apparently an important question: What zodiac sign was I? This should have been a giveaway. Do people actually think the alignment of planets and stars have an effect on our personalities? It was outright hogwash to me, but I let it slide. "I'm a Gemini" I said. Unbeknownst to me at the time, two Gemini spelled trouble. I was not, however, about to argue with Apkins one way or another about what I considered to be outright rubbish.

Our first date was fun. We went to In-N-Out Burger. Our conversation was fun and easy, but what stuck out to me was what Apkins insisted on doing to her soda. She got a Coke, and asked an employee if they had any lemon slices. The patron pointed to where the fruit was accessible next to the fountain drinks. She headed over and squeezed all the juice out of a slice into her open cup. This wasn't abnormal. I too enjoyed a little acidic charge to my Coca-Cola. But then she did it again with another slice, then again, then once more, then again. She repeated this eleven times. The whole ordeal probably took three minutes.

When we got back to her apartment we started playing Phase 10, a fairly simple card game. Apkins' roommate and boyfriend were there with us. Her roommate Rita was corpulent and tremendously profane. She claimed that being a Boston native was the reason for her unedited speech, but I had other theories. I can handle the occasional curse word or crude joke, but Rita's excuse for a mouth spewed endless torrents of insults and expletives seemingly laced with absinthe. Even her muskrat of a boyfriend looked sheepish when she spoke.

I judged Apkins a little bit for being friends with such an individual, but then I remembered not all of my friends were perfectly domesticated and suitable for social interactions. Some people were your friends for no better reason than because they were your friends.

Disgusting Rita aside, our card game was pretty enjoyable and Apkins seemed to be sitting closer and closer to me with each round that passed. What happened next again was a sign of crazy, but I dismissed it as a natural bodily function. She farted. Flatulence is acceptable, we all do it. But she did not seem embarrassed in the least. She saw that I had heard her misdeed and simply tossed her hair back and laughed as if she had just said *buttfinger* instead of Butterfinger. I wasn't sure what to think of it. I reasoned with myself that she was just confident and secure with her own body.

The next clue of insanity came a week or two later when we were eating with some friends at a Chinese restaurant. We happened to be on a group date with some married friends of mine, a more austere group than Apkins was probably used to. We ate without any real incident, but every couple of minutes someone would say something remotely funny and Apkins would erupt. It was not a laugh; it was a loud cackle that sounded painful and terrifying. It was like she was going through puberty while screaming at the top of her lungs. It was menacing and likely made a few children in the booth next to us cry.

Despite the slightly mortifying public guffawing, I was starting to really like this girl. That night we kissed for the first time. It wasn't amazing, but again her level of attractiveness obscured the reasoning sections of my brain, making me think our kiss was stellar.

Over the next few weeks we hung out sporadically. Her behavior was maddeningly unpredictable. One day she would be all over me with a sensuality bordering on the deviant, the next day she would completely flake on me, not answering her phone or replying to my texts. She was erratic and confusing to no end. After a few weeks of this I was determined to put an end to the madness. I made ultimatums that I would have easily backed out of, but they didn't seem to bother Apkins. She seemed increasingly concerned with our incompatibility that she surmised was due to us both being Gemini.

I could not reason with this broad. I should have ended things myself, but instead I held on to the hope that she would get over her weird beliefs. She did not. One night in a desperate attempt to hang out with her, I received a text that sent me into a whirlwind of despair.

I was just trying to weasel my way into seeing her that night, because she was giving me bogus excuses. I would tell her that I just wanted to see her and that it could be as brief as she wanted. My texts that were sent in triplicate must have sent her over the edge. She finally responded, telling me in no uncertain terms that she did not want to date me and that she simply did not see us going anywhere. My normal reaction would be to argue my case, or at least try to find the underlying reason for my dismissal. But I opted to just respond with the letter K.

I had to go for a walk. As always, I was in no mood to explain to my male friends why I was crying. The fact that I was crying over a girl I had only known for a few weeks infuriated me. How could I be so sensitive and obtuse? It was summer now and I walked a half mile or so to a nearby indoor sports complex that was well abandoned at that time of night. I sat beneath a flood light and cried louder than I probably ever have as an adult. No one was within sight or sound of me, so I let myself go in the ugliest conceivable fashion. Salty tears and snot poured out of my face onto the gum-filled concrete.

I don't think I was so inconsolably forlorn just because of Apkins. I think things had added up over the past year and they were all being released at once. I sat there and bellowed inside and out, thinking about my failed relationships, failures in school and overall lack of prosperity. It is amazing how when you are unraveling emotionally every single negative aspect of your life appears to be physically placed in your lap, while a nonexistent crowd proceeds to point and laugh at you. It is all very overdramatized, but it feels real and it feels horrible. The reality of things was that my life was great.

I had a wonderful family, a decent job, supportive friends and women liked me, even if their interest piqued quickly. But those things didn't matter at that moment. When you are lamenting your own life, you don't consider the fortuitous and blessed elements of your existence, you focus on the bleak and the impossible.

I got over Apkins very quickly, but that night was awful. A phone call later that night with my father really put things in perspective. After a few hours of tears, hair pulling and self-pity I finally limped out of my dark crawlspace in the search of light. And Dad always provided light. Not only would he laugh with me, and give me advice, he would cry with me. Even on the phone I could feel his powerful empathy. Even if he hadn't experienced exactly what I had, he sure made me feel like he had, and not in a dishonest way, but a comforting way.

My next sweetheart was another dragged out, painful and as always, avoidable mess. Our relationship was never even a relationship. It was a series of spurned advances and hurtful chicanery. Cooper was not the malicious type, just another confused girl that didn't deal with her fickleness in a very compassionate way.

We had a few weeks of disjointed meet-ups and almost- kisses. I mistakenly thought not kissing Cooper initially would make her want me more. It had the opposite effect; the night we nearly kissed was the closest I ever got. But this did not stop me from wasting months talking to her and assuming she would come around. It seemed that with each failed relationship I was learning less and less. I should have at least been gathering bits and pieces of knowledge about the female gender; instead it appeared that I was simply compiling fodder for future screw-ups.

Cooper and I managed to remain amicable after months of cold hellos and unwanted side-hugs. She was a lovely person that loved the person I was, but didn't love me. There was nothing especially wrong with me; she just didn't want to be with me. I could understand this. There were multitudes of women I loved being around, loved kissing but with whom I had no visions of longevity. This was the reality of dating. It was often very cut and dry, even obvious, but the reasons no matter the logic, hurt, and they hurt in a way that was just as physical as it was mental.

The last couple of years had awarded me many nights of victory, many entangled relationships and a handful of pseudo girlfriends. What I never actually had post-high school was a girlfriend, an actual inamorata.

I met Timmons in a crowded place. I actually noticed her not because of her outstanding beauty but because of her little group. She was with her two sisters and her mother. Her mother was in her late forties and not exactly a female heartthrob, but she was not ugly. Her two sisters were in high school, but from a distance all I saw was a clan of brunette wonders. It's never easy to approach a pretty girl when she is surrounded by people, especially when those people are family, but I had to do something. I was with my buddy Bryce, and we contrived a ruse. We would pretend we needed a third party to take our picture for us. I approached the intimidating group of well-dressed and finely groomed women and grabbed my target, motioning towards Bryce and our need for photographic expertise. She coyly followed me, took our picture and handed back my phone. Before I grabbed it I said "Since you already have my phone, why don't you just put your number in it." She smiled, acquiesced and was off before we could exchange much else.

Our first date was the next weekend. After a little get-to-know-you texting I found out she lived two hours away from me. Normally this would have been an immediate deterrent, but I was lonely and fed up with things not working out. I had decent gas mileage, and long-distance relationships had worked countless times in movies. We decided to meet half-way between our residences. Before I even saw her I decided I had to go big, I had to deliver. If it was a mediocre date neither of us would feel inclined to drive two hours for a second date. I had to kiss her. This was a risky plan, but I figured I didn't have much to lose.

We met for an ethnic dinner that was followed by a pleasant stroll through a modern art museum and then a nightcap of hot chocolate. The night was fairly routine from the onset. Timmons was moderately shy and you could tell interest was present, but not much else. After our warm drinks we started walking back to our cars. I'm not sure which cosmic genius had directed this scene, but they had called for rain. It was an April downpour that was not too cold but that quickly produced puddles. We had been walking arm in arm, but mere seconds after the clouds let go of their raindrops our arms dropped to our sides and our hands seemed to gently collide. Timmons' thumb started caressing the base of my thumb and my skin popped with goose bumps. After some playful puddle-hopping we arrived back at her car. Kissing her had been on my mind the entire night, but now it was time to execute.

We leaned against her car and talked for several minutes, the type of speech that revealed no real information, but simply filled the empty space before the next scene. I kept creeping closer to her face, wanting her to lean in, making it easier for me, but she did not. She also didn't shy away, so I finally tightened the noose on my fear and kissed her. At first her face clenched like it wasn't sure what was happening, but then she kissed back. She smelled like a bowl of strawberries, but the kiss was uncouth and second-rate. I favor the bottom lip, and she seemed to like it the other way around. We kissed for about twenty seconds before we both surrendered. She wasn't a bad kisser; we both just clearly were used to kissing different people.

My entire drive home I couldn't decide how well the date had gone. I think Timmons was a little reluctant to kiss me on our first outing, but I had to go big. There was no time for amateur efforts.

Our next couples of dates were in the same city, equidistant from her place and mine. The kissing improved as did the flow of conversation. We were working on neutral ground, so we resorted to making out in her car like two illicit lovers dodging the eyes of their parents. Our planned activities became nothing more than excuses to see each other and be intimate. I liked Timmons without really knowing why. She was very easy going and had a cute shyness about her. I myself was more outgoing and I guess I was a bit intoxicated by the balance we had.

The distance between us was a glaring problem that neither one of us was ready to address, so we kept it in a locked cellar. What was the big deal? We both had keys to this cellar and could access it whenever we pleased.

Our relationship was dictated by the weekend. Each Friday or Saturday we would take turns driving, one week to my place, the next to hers. Besides the distance, everything was going well. We hadn't even required a conversation to officialize our exclusivity. It simply arrived one day like the wind. It isn't windy every day, but when it is you don't think much of it. Timmons was beautiful and uncomplicated. I could envision a life with her. There was only one issue that stood in front of us, and I was the only one who could see it.

Timmons still lived with her parents. Not only was she living at home, but she had never lived anywhere else. She lived in the same residence where she took her first steps. She had never dealt with the dichotomy of roommates that didn't share her DNA. She was unfamiliar with living with boys for the most part. Her immediate family consisted of her, her parents and her three sisters. The only male presence in her life was her Yankee-loving pushover of a father. This worried me. She didn't understand or react to teasing the way I was used to, and she couldn't fathom a separation between her and her fraternal twin sister. She felt an enormous obligation to watch out for her mildly rebellious sister who was younger by way of minutes.

I could sympathize with all of this, my problem was I was searching for marriage, for companionship and I worried that a nineteen year old who had never left her comfy nest and who still had no idea what she wanted to do with life was not a very safe choice. She was the opposite of a flight risk. She was a stationary risk. I feared that she never wanted to leave her white trash-adjacent neighborhood and the comfort of her slightly younger sister.

I secretly entered that locked cellar and gingerly placed my concerns about Timmons' immaturity next to the distance quagmire. She wouldn't have to know I had crept down there to hide more of my worries. She had probably made her way down there at some point to conceal her own preoccupations.

Timmons and I had been happily dating for two months. We saw each other as much as we could, never fought and even met each other's families. But Christmas was approaching and this left me with an uneasy feeling in my stomach. Don't get me wrong, I love presents, gleeful photo-ops and endless feasts; but I knew that Christmas was an unspoken breaking point in many relationships. You don't want to get extravagant gifts for a significant other if things are rocky at best. You don't want to spend time away from your family if you think your relationship only has another two or three weeks left until it expires. On top of that there is the possibility of spending an entire fortnight away from your girlfriend. That is too much space, too much time if things are at all fragile. I was right. Christmas of 2012 murdered my relationship with Timmons. I would be a Grinch and blame the whole essence of yuletide tradition in ruining something precious, but it was just coincidence. Christmas actually helped us see what wasn't there. We both loved being around each other, but did not love each other.

We went the whole Christmas vacation without seeing each other. I saw her one last time on December 18th before I went home. But we didn't see each other again until December 30th. At this point our lack of communication had well outlined for us the nature of our next encounter. Unlike she had in times past, Timmons drove down to my place with zero plans in motion for the night. We hadn't discussed dinner, a movie or any other form of recreation. It was implicit what was going to happen. A black horse was on its way from a neighboring village with news already known. Alas, you wait for the messenger even if the incoming message will be of no surprise.

Timmons walked into my apartment as sullen as I had ever seen her. Instead of grabbing my hand and joining me to my room like we usually did, she briskly walked ahead of me. We sat on my bed and I could feel a deep sadness emanating from both of us. I put my hand on her leg. I immediately felt it was the wrong move, but I felt awkward removing it so quickly.

To preface what would be a painful and unorganized chat, Timmons pulled out a wrapped gift from her large purse. It was my Christmas present. I was 99% sure we were going to break up, so I hadn't purchased her a single item. I didn't even have a nice card with a few words scribbled over it. I had nothing. What a chump. Timmons had given me a leather-bound journal. I was almost through with my previous mole-skin journal so it was exactly what I needed and no one else had thought of such a thing for me that

Christmas. As I looked at it, I started making up a story about how her gift was on lay-away. She knew I was bluffing, but didn't care. "I got this for you like a month ago, so don't worry about it." She had left an inscription on the first leaf of the journal saying,

"Taylor, Merry Christmas! I hope you have a good holiday with your family. I know you are exchanging sentimental gifts with your family…and this is as close as I can get. I love writing in journals, and I know that you do, too. (I know, I'm so original.) But this one I really love because of the scripture on the front. It's perfect. I think everything in life happens for a reason, every experience teaches us and helps us grow as people. Every person we meet is meant to be a lesson in some way. (Good or bad.) Writing these things down…Well I know I don't have to preach to you about that. Just use this journal when you need a new one, I hope you can write mostly happy things. Merry Christmas, and have a great 2013."

Besides her erroneous uses of ellipses and superfluous commas I thought it was pretty nice. But it had the personal touch of a cousin, maybe a longtime neighbor, not a girlfriend. In a way it was the perfect adieu. It wasn't sappy and nostalgic. To me it basically read, "Taylor, you are a good guy, I hope life works out for you, no hard feelings. Happy Jesus Day."

We sat on my bed, journal on the floor, wondering what words needed to be said. We both said a few words and before I realized it, Timmons popped up tautly and said "I think I'm gonna go." "Can I walk you to your car?" I asked. "No, it's ok."

We hugged, and I pushed tears back into my face with some force I didn't know I had. She walked out and headed down the stairs. I would never see her again. I returned to my room with a strange mixture of anger and sadness. I couldn't sit, I was pacing like a wide-eyed professor on the cusp of some scientific breakthrough. But there was no breakthrough to be had. I looked at my bedroom door and felt rage swim through my veins. Without further thought I hurled my fist into it as hard as I could. Luckily for my knuckles and novice punching hand the door was hollow and made of cheap soft wood. Damage to my paw and the door were minimal. I was surprised at how upset I was. Timmons and I had kind of drifted apart before we ever managed to drift together. I shouldn't have been too torn up, but I was. It is not easy breaking up with someone you care about. Just because it doesn't make sense anymore doesn't mitigate your feelings towards them. They are still a person you cared about and thought about.

The very next night was New Year's Eve and I was in no mood to pretend like I could dance, or to procure a suitable kissing mate for midnight. But my buddies were not going to accept my morose state as an excuse for not partying. No way. We headed out and I managed to find a girl or two to kiss at midnight. Even though I was uncharacteristically gloomy, girls seemed to find it charming. I wasn't sweating profusely or dancing obscenely, so I suppose I had a leg-up on the other vultures. The night turned out to be a marginal success, and it helped me forget about my fresh wound.

A few days later, determined to get over the mess of emotions that tugged at my heartstrings, I returned to old flames. When an experienced hunter is feeling down on himself, he doesn't seek new and rare prey, he slaughters pigeons. Easy killing. That's what I wanted. My heart was bummed out and I couldn't stand to spend my nights alone. So, I went through my phone and hit up girls that I hadn't talked to in years. Surprisingly, some had either forgiven me, forgotten what had happened between us, or rather fancied my new hairstyle. It was a new year, and I was happy to start it off with a pow.

Little did I know that 2013 would prove to be an awful and generally forgettable year. It started off okay. I met lots of new people and was enjoying the end of basketball season. But the Timmons episode had stuck with me and left me bothered. Part of me was disturbed that I was so affected by a girl I had courted for only two months, a girl that *I* had broken up with. It was mutual. But I was miserable. I was disenchanted with everything around me. School was becoming something I didn't want to finish. Girls once again became objects, and my continual procrastination became more than just tendency. I neglected my homework. I didn't call friends back, and I didn't pay my speeding tickets. I created a fictional world in my head where things were crappy, but where they all eventually worked themselves out. The problem with my delusion was that I never made a plan as to how these snafus would be solved.

So, in the next six months I found to my dismay that I had failed my classes and ran up a considerable amount of debt. My car had been unregistered for months now and I was driving around with a constant paranoia that I would get pulled over. I already had several tickets which I had not paid and one more citation was going to end badly for me.

I was stuck in what at the time felt like an impossible catch-22. In order to get my car registered I had to repair a few things so it would pass inspection, but I didn't have the money to repair those things. To get more money I obviously needed to work more, but work required me driving quite a bit which augmented the possibility of getting pulled over, a consequence I couldn't risk. So, what was my grand solution to this problem? Do nothing. I ducked my head and desperately ran around hoping nothing would hit me. The problem with this method is it will often work for a while. This tends to give you the false notion that you are invincible. You know that isn't really true, but you don't allow yourself to entertain such perfidious thoughts.

The next couple of months were a perpetual routine of hanging out with new girls, often until the wee-hours of the morning, sleeping in till way past noon, eating out every meal and working occasionally. It wasn't the worst way to live. I was having fun, was moderately happy and even had a job. I was caring less and less about girls that had left my heart in tangled disarray, and was generally abstemious from addictive things. Life wasn't exactly a plum, but it wasn't so bad.

One night I was spending some time with Aubrey, a girl I was quite fond of. We weren't moving towards Seriousville, but we were having a fetching good time. I left her place that night at close to four in the morning. I was tired, but starving. I had to go get a little snack of some sort before I went home. How was I to know that my hunger would ultimately turn around and with sharpened cleats unmercifully kick me in the jaw?

I drove to the Maverick gas station a few miles down the road, determined to get a Cheddarwurst. Right as I pulled up I noticed a cop car parked in the darkness across the street. Surely there wouldn't be a problem. It was freakishly late and the officer certainly would have better things to do than to scope down my license plate and see if my stickers were current. But just in case, I loitered about in the gas station for longer than usual before returning to my car. I hopped in my Kia Spectra and pulled out of the parking lot slowly. I hung a right and immediately saw the police car behind me. He was following me, but hadn't turned on his lights. I approached a stoplight and knew only a miracle would spare me from being pulled over. I blinked left, my eyes not deviating from my rearview mirror. His lights still weren't on. Maybe fortune had arrived at my doorstep. The traffic light switched and I turned left. Blue and red. There would be no semblance of luck that night.

The officer came to my window and I knew I would receive a ticket, an egregious one at that. He took my information and returned to his vehicle to do whatever it is that policemen do in that situation. For all I know they are looking up traffic laws or texting their mothers, maybe finishing a Sudoku game. Whatever it is they do, it always takes an inappropriate amount of time. This stop was no exception. The copper returned to my window, his face wiped clean of any friendliness that was there before. "We are going to have to impound your car" he said tersely. As he went through the other obligatory words of protocol, I heard nothing. Just like a convicted felon only hears the word guilty, he does not hear the proceeding words detailing the sentence.

I got out of my car and fumed silently on the curb. At some point another unit showed up, as if two officers would not be ample muscle for a guy like me. I remained defeated on the curb while one of them called a tow truck and the other three swapped exaggerated stories about traffic stops.

I was about a mile from home, with no car, and it was pretty chilly. The law enforcers had offered to give me a ride home, but the last thing I wanted to do was spend another second with those vermin. It's like getting beat to a pulp, knocked unconscious, and then waking up to your assailant asking you if you would like to join him for an ice cream cone. Their politeness offended me. I called the only person who I knew would be awake and willing to drive me home, Aubrey.

Aubrey zoomed over to my sedentary location. I could see she was wrought with concern and sympathy. I was nothing but embarrassed. How could I be so unbelievably negligent? I could barely look at Aubrey on the ride home. She kept talking, trying to ease my mind, but all I could think about was how I couldn't afford the couple hundred dollars it would take to remove my car from the towing yard the next day. I had a couple hundred dollars to my name, but rent was due in a couple days, as was my phone bill.

We pulled up to my apartment and I kissed Aubrey long and good. Not because I was crazy about her and thankful for her timely gesture, but because I didn't want to think about anything else. My state of being carefree lasted the duration of the kiss, then I went inside. I wanted to sleep until I was twenty-nine.

The next four weeks I was in a perpetual state of financial panic. I couldn't ask my parents for money, and I couldn't make money without a means of transportation. So, I borrowed my grandparents' green van. It was not known for its sexual magnetism, but it was helpful. I was able to get some work done, earn a few hundred extra dollars, pay my rent, my phone bill and take care of a couple amenities. But I still didn't have enough money to get my car out of the tow yard, and apparently it cost twenty dollars a day to keep my vehicle behind a chain-linked fence.

After a couple more weeks of money-borrowing and pride swallowing I had gathered enough moolah to retrieve my baby from the despotic tow yard. I called the towing agency to see what time they closed, so I could get my car that night or the next day. The man who answered the phone sounded like a person I would not like. Maybe it was his position, his part in my tragedy, but I think it was his voice. He sounded uneducated and bothered as if I had knocked on his door incessantly during a family dinner. "What kind of car do you have?" he asked in an unpleasant tone. "An 04' Kia Spectra, silver" I said. There was silence while he presumably looked in the system for my car. "That was sold at auction yesterday" he said nonchalantly. This was not my most articulate moment. I stuttered rapidly into the receiver with words like huh, whuh, why, what, ugh, um, splattered with some choice vulgarity.

This man who had now become the cause of my misfortune apathetically explained their policies and my lack of options. I said something rude and hung up. I had stepped outside to make the phone call because I like to pace when I am on the phone; it makes me feel like I'm accomplishing something at the same time. This specific telephone conversation had taken me four or five blocks from my apartment, and miles from sanity. I felt like screaming and punching, all of the emotions of a disgruntled toddler overcame my body and mind. I was furious with this fascist towing company and the ruthless policemen. But honestly the fury was aimed mostly at myself. I had messed up, and though I blamed others, I knew it was my doing.

Sure they have finance, accounting, and economy classes in high school, even home economics. But they do not have any class entitled *How to Avoid Screwing Up in Life*. Nor do they have the follow-up course *How to Deal With Your Now Screwed Up Life*. No teacher had ever told me "Now Taylor when you inevitably get your car impounded make sure to get it out within thirty days so said vehicle is not sold at auction."

I now had no car, no money, no girl, and had recently learned that enrolling in school in the fall would not be an option. I owed too much money on my student loans. The one good thing about having all of life's problems attack you at once is that you no longer have one all-consuming tragedy defining your existence, you now have a cornucopia of dilemmas that all kind of blur together in a sort of monochromatic Rubik's cube.

I was once again rudderless and things looked bleaker than they ever had. I knew life could be much worse, but when life hasn't handed you much in the means of tragedy and hardship, the trivial blows seem catastrophic. Part of you feels guilty for complaining about your tiny problems, but at the end of the day they are still problems and if they are the biggest problems you have ever had, they will likewise be the hardest ones to solve and get past.

For a few weeks I sulked and slept too much. I drove myself crazy at night trying to sleep. All I could think about were my bills stacking up and my complete lack of progression in life. I wasn't depressed, but I feared depression was on its way to my house and would bully its way through the front door.

One night I tried everything I could think of to fall asleep; I read, I watched movies, but ultimately I just laid there. Nothing worked. The sun started coming up and I was not remotely tired. My thoughts would not allow my body to rest. I decided I needed to do something to invigorate myself, release myself from the dungeon I had exiled myself to. It was now seven o'clock in the morning. I put on my tennis shoes and decided to go for a run. Now let's remember something about me: I am athletic, I've played sports my entire life. I am in great shape and good health. But I do not run for pleasure. This idea of jogging by yourself, with no one timing you, with no one trying to catch you, seemed counterproductive and an overall waste of shoe tread. But I had to peer outside of the box here.

I grabbed my iPod, my phone and jogged down the stairs into my parking lot. I had no idea where I was going or how long I was going to run. I was just running because I literally couldn't think of a better activity. I needed catharsis, and so many Facebook statuses had raved about the solace and "peace of mind" found on these runs.

My neighborhood sat at the foot of a rather large mountain. It was probably half a mile to the base. Me being however somewhat of an indoorsman, I was not at all familiar with the paths and functions of a mountain in the summertime. I knew it was a runner's paradise, but I was no runner.

I ran to the base and arrived only mildly out of breath. I ran up an inclined path at a rather slow pace until I noticed a makeshift shelter twenty yards from me that was clearly a homeless man's camping spot. It is hard to get a good read on the indigent, so I ran a little faster. The road winded and my thoughts were clearer than they had been in months. I was breathing some new brand of air, and my lungs were pleased with the freshness. I was in no condition, nor did I have any desire to reach the summit. I just wanted a slightly more elevated spot where I could stop, ponder and enjoy the vista. I ran at five minute intervals then walked for thirty seconds while my pulse returned to a more normal pace.

I noticed a large rock just off the path that would be easy enough to scale. I jumped over some briars and climbed the natural edifice. As was my hope, there was a beautiful view of the city below. I could see my apartment complex just down the street and the lake five miles away. Was this why people hiked? Certainly it couldn't be for any other purpose. I carefully selected the right playlist on my iPod that would be conducive for introspective reflection.

As I sat there, sweaty and tired, I contemplated my failures. I tried to eliminate any thoughts of negativity that swirled around me. I don't know how long I stayed there before I made my descent, but it was time well spent. I spoke at great length with myself and with my Creator. With my eyes closed, perched on a mossy rock, I discovered what was probably obvious to everyone else around me. I came to the realization that fecal matter had hit the fan, but so what? All I had to do was cover my nose and start cleaning. My attitude had to change. Sure the process of cleaning crap off the walls would be arduous and unpleasant, but what else was I going to do? Just avoid the poop-filled room and go about my life while things festered underneath the door?

I headed back down to my place, choosing a different and longer path. When I got home I was exhausted, but imbued with the type of energy that overrides sleepiness. I started making goals and outlines for my future success. It would take some time to recover financially from the hole I had dug myself, but I would be okay. I realized that coaching basketball that upcoming season would be out of the question. A small stipend would not get me where I needed to be. I was blessed to have a job that allowed me to work virtually when and wherever I wanted, and I needed to take advantage of that for once.

Along with a few other mini epiphanies, while amidst the fowl and fresh air, I decided I needed to write more. I had started a blog a few months before, but had been doing it for the sole purpose of quelling my own creative constipation. I wasn't thinking of making a career out of it, or aspiring to get published. But I had received a lot of positive feedback from my posts, so maybe it was time to do something more with my creative juices.

I increased the frequency of my blog posts and decided I needed to write books. I read on a blog for writers that "those 'aspiring to be writers' should stop calling themselves aspiring writers or amateur writers and should henceforth call themselves writers, for if you write, you are a writer." So I started to research and procure topics for my hypothetical books. I was still broke, still relatively lonely and still bereft of wheels, but things were moving forward, the quality of life was improving.

As was my custom at this point, I met another girl. This time our story was a little less romantic. We met via a new dating app. I was a couple hours away from home, working, and I was bored. Our profiles matched up and I messaged her. She was enthusiastic and agreed to come over and meet me at my friend's house I was staying at. But it was already after midnight. The common pleasantries that go hand-in-hand with meeting someone around dinner time seem rather superfluous after a certain hour. When it is late no one wants to sit in a chair and discuss hobbies. You want to lie down, you want to be comfortable, and you don't want to worry about how finely coiffed your hair is.

Hill lightly knocked on the door and we embraced before ever saying a word to each other. Hill was tall, very thin, yet athletic. She was a collegiate soccer player and donned blue jeans that appeared to be painted on, and Chuck Taylor's. We scuttled back to the guestroom to "watch a movie." But who yearns for cinematic entertainment in the middle of the night? We actually got through the entire film before we kissed. But once the kissing started, it didn't stop until the sun had made its warm welcome.

There are myriad forms of kissing, but when it comes to passionate kissing, the kind that gets sloppy and requires extra oxygen, there are two types. They are both likely to produce a good time, but the first is more of a routine sort of recreation; it is fun, but nothing special. It is exciting, but just a notch above being platonic. The second form of kissing mirrors the first in every physical aspect, but for some unknown reason it becomes chemical. It becomes much more than a monotonous flinching of facial muscles, and metamorphoses into an unexplainable force of kinetic energy. The kissing that was had between Hill and I that night was of the latter nature. It's like our faces were soul mates.

Alas, Hill lived some four hours from me. And that wasn't the only obstacle. We had completely contrasting religious views. Now for some people a lack of spiritual accord in a relationship is about as consequential as soda preference. If a lover of Pepsi can be with a Coca-Cola enthusiast then a Catholic and a Protestant should be able to make it work. But religion held a little more importance to me.

I hadn't felt such a caliber of passion with a girl since Lilly, so it was very disheartening to meet a girl that aroused my faculties so, just to find out a relationship would be virtually impossible. On top of that, Hill was crazy about me. Now I have had a handful of girls that were absolutely and unexplainably bonkers about me, but usually it is somewhat of a turn off. Hill, however flattered me to no end, and I loved it.

In the following months we both made an effort to see each other in our respective cities. We talked frequently and never quarreled. Of course we avoided at all costs the topics that were difficult. But we both dated other people, and knew that what we had wouldn't last. It was like viewing the Northern Lights; it was beautiful, even breathtaking at moments, and for lack of a better word, magical. Alas, it was fleeting and we both were very aware of it. But you don't watch the Aurora Borealis while discussing its brevity, you enjoy it. You take in the stunning vista and let the auroral colors consume you. That's what Hill and I did for some time. We met up maybe five or six times before it became too much.

We were expending too much energy into something we both knew was doomed.

Our relationship sadly gave up the ghost over a series of text messages. As amorous as things had felt, we both knew it was an over-romanticized fling. We had no hard feelings and both understood that in a different time with just a few details changed, we would have been together. There is both solace and frustration in a notion like this. It is comforting that we both chose to go in another direction, but it hurts to know we simply gave up because it was hard, or seemed undoable. The disquiet I felt came mostly from the fact that I so rarely felt this way about a girl. It was like finding a small diamond on a dirt road, and then misplacing it. Losing the diamond is so distressing because you know how unlikely it is to find another rock so precious. Pebbles and muddied stones were all over, but they lacked any real value and often crumbled with ease. I knew there were other wonderful stones out there, but I knew it would not be easy to find another one.

Ch. 7- What's Next?

"It's amazing how a little tomorrow can make up for a whole lot of yesterday." ~ John Guare

December 17, 2013

That night my oldest friend Ryan and I got in the car and drove forty-five minutes until we reached a neighborhood with small brick homes and shoveled sidewalks. We found a spot on the street that would likely result in a parking violation and exited the car. It was freezing outside and I was glad to be wearing my nicest pea coat. We were attending a Christmas dinner party. I knew exactly two people attending this festive soiree, and one of them I had arrived with. The other known attendee was Lauren, a girl I barely knew; one of those people that you could not for the life of you remember if you had met just once or four or five times. It was her gathering, and she was the one who invited Ryan and me. She was nice and pleasant enough, but Ryan and I had previously determined without vacillation that the party would be a drag. We would make a courtesy showing, and then bail the moment we were not pleased with the atmosphere.

In the Facebook invitation it was specified that there would be a dress-code. Women were to wear dresses or long skirts while the gents were required to sport button-ups with ties. I had no intention of showing up in formal wear to what I considered a very informal get together. To not look like a complete heathen, I wore a buttoned up shirt (untucked) , black skinny jeans and my best pair of brown leather boots, which also happened to be my only pair of shoes that contained any semblance of brown or leather.

We knocked on the door that had clearly been there for decades, shivering and dreading the contents of the evening at hand. Lauren answered the door with an overly jovial reception and rushed us in. We quickly noticed that not another male was in sight, and only three other girls were visible. Was this some sort of ruse to awkwardly pair up lonely women with unsuspecting men?

Lauren assured us that everyone was running late, and that in the meantime we should make ourselves comfortable. Well, I was already uncomfortable. Three girls dressed to the nines were putting the finishing touches on the victuals. I was soon assigned to put garnish on one of the platters. I felt ill-prepared for this job since I had only recently learned what garnish even was. But I did my best to arrange the throw pillows of the cooking world around some unknown metal holding device. While I tended to my garnish and tried not to look like I was too cool for what I was doing, people started to trickle in.

This was a different crowd. The men wore bowties and framed ocular accessories without prescriptions. The women had bright red lipstick and gaudy dresses. Thirty minutes had passed since we arrived and I was ready to feed. The majority of the guests were there and I was disappointed. I could not believe we still hadn't started dinner, but also I was annoyed that we drove nearly an hour and there was but one attractive girl in the entire residence. I thought dinner parties were about meeting sophisticated and fancy members of society, but all I saw were the dregs of single adulthood.

The one noteworthy dame there was too shy and too swarmed by overeager men in their late twenties to even be approachable. I fought and pushed for a few sentences with her, but my locutions likely resonated with her as much as an "I appreciated your speech" comment by a lowly bystander would stick with the President of the United States. Any further effort with this girl would be moot.

I decided to just enjoy the food and text people I deemed more important while I sipped my sparkling soda. As I sat by myself in a hard plastic chair with sub-par lumber support, Ryan darted from conversation to conversation like a gregarious pinball. This was Ryan's scene. He loved meeting new people, no matter how hipster, how pedantic or how mind-numbingly boring they might be. He loved to network and play the name game with people. I liked soda and beautiful women. I wasn't pouting, but I probably looked like it. I was now leaning back in my chair against the wall, looking at my phone and avoiding any potential communication with the other guests.

Lauren came and sat by me, asking me how I was enjoying the party. I lied with a believable smile, telling her how delicious the food was and how delightful the people were. Lauren was savvy though. "Not really your cup of tea, huh?"

I tried to remain polite while not being completely full of crap. "I'm just tired, and not super interested in talking to people I will never see again." She sincerely accepted my retort and we continued to chat. It turns out Lauren was a pretty intelligent girl.

She worked at Goldman Sachs and was a history major just like I was. We started to talk about a book concerning the history of salt. Ironically I had thought the group that night was collectively pretty dull, but there I was discussing with great animation historical misnomers about sodium.

Mid-conversation the front door opened and a couple entered the dining room hand in hand. They were absolutely gorgeous. I couldn't take my eyes off of either of them. The guy had the height of a collegiate basketball player, with the hair of a European soccer star. Normally when I see a guy with a beautiful girl on his arm I instantly assume he is a tool and a scoundrel that doesn't deserve such a creature. But this dude had this infectious swagger about him. He was cool, and I simultaneously wanted to be his best friend and pilfer his girlfriend.

The girl was something out of the movies. She had a smile that persisted even when she wasn't talking with or looking at anyone. She couldn't have been over five feet tall, but she was so absurdly attractive that you didn't notice how short she was until you had admired the rest of her, and there was much to admire. Her hair was the color of some dark wood I had never seen before. Her eyes were big and kind. Her body was five-star. But what I couldn't keep my eyes off of was her face. You hear people talk about natural beauty, and the kind of beauty that makes you look twice. This was a hybrid of the two, with an extra portion of regal appeal. Her nose was hand-crafted by the gods, made with a kind of cartilage this world has never seen. Her skin was a light brown tone, hinting at an ambiguous ethnic background. Her features captivated me to no end. I finally knew how Adam felt when God placed Eve in the garden with him, for it was as if I was seeing the female species for the very first time.

I tried not to stare, but I didn't try very hard. I had nothing to lose. She clearly didn't live very close to me, and was dating someone that was obviously related to Zeus. So, what else could I do? I shamefully ogled this woman, fantasizing that she would find me enigmatically handsome and approachable. Surely she would seductively accost me confessing to me the unhappy state of her relationship. I would undoubtedly say the perfect words that would push her over the edge. She would consequently break up with her

Greek god and go home with me. This leviathan man would congratulate and even raise a glass to me and my new prize, a real class act.

The fantasy swiftly and mercilessly disappeared like a fallen contact lens in a crowded venue. From a distance I watched her laugh and caress his arm following what had to have been a magnificently told anecdote. I stopped staring and chalked it up as a loss. She certainly wasn't the first stunning and unattainable woman I had seen or met in my life.

The rest of the night felt vacuous and unsatisfying. I motioned to Ryan that it was time for us to leave, then I sat down, knowing he would take fifteen or twenty minutes to wrap up all the loose ends of his scattered conversations. The girl whose name I didn't even catch had already left with her flawless counterpoint. I waited patiently, grabbed a can of soda for the road and wondered if I would ever run across that ravishing girl again. We were nearly the last ones to leave the party. The night turned out to be more enjoyable than I had originally anticipated, but I felt oddly empty inside. I scolded myself for not even trying to talk to this girl. You never know when somebody's relationship is on the rocks. Why not be the subtle catalyst in a breakup? Why not be a quiet reminder that there are still good men walking around? My own hypotheticals held no weight since I imagined her boyfriend to be nearly as perfect as she was.

Ryan and I drove home, listening to electronica music and talking about college basketball. Cars wisped by and as the night came to an end, so did my delusions that I would ever see that girl again. I hadn't even gotten her name. I had nothing.

A few days later I drove home in the snow for Christmas break. I loved this time of year. I loathed the frigid temperatures, but everything else was glorious. I would spend nearly two weeks engorging myself with food, literature and libations. My parents lived in a rural town with a population of 2,256. Christmas time meant no girls. Any girls in that town were married, jailbait, or fond of methamphetamines. So, I hung out with my family and guys I played sports with in high school. I didn't even bother texting anyone from "up north" during the break since cell reception was spotty and I didn't have any legitimate female interests at the time.

Since both of my sisters were married, I didn't even get to sleep in my own room. I was banished to the dark and cold basement. Besides having very low ceilings and the necessity for more blankets, it wasn't so bad. The room I slept in was windowless and not unlike a cave. I could sleep well past lunch down there without even realizing it. There had to be some benefits to not having a significant other. The couples got the nicer mattresses, but I got unencumbered sleep; no untimely rays of sunshine or sounds of crunching cereal.

One night after countless hours of trivia games and snacking with the family I retired to my bat-cave, and only emerged eleven hours later. When I came upstairs I overheard talk about dinner preparations. I still had breakfast on the mind. I sat down at the kitchen table and looked through my phone. I opened up Instagram to see the festive pictures and clever hashtags I had missed over the last few days. I noticed Lauren had posted a picture, but it was still loading. I put it on the table and poured myself some juice. When I picked up my phone I saw the picture. It was her, the angelic being from the Christmas dinner party I had all but forgotten about.

I immediately became giddy like a little kid that just discovered his birthday would now be celebrated tri-annually. I tapped on her Instagram handle, leading me to her profile. I had discovered she possessed a name, adding a pinch of reality to the fairytale I had created. Her last name was Child. I looked at all 193 of her posts. I even double-tapped a few, then realized I needed to follow her. My mind started summersaulting. Child would see that I followed her. Would she remember me from the party? Would she find an unsolicited "follow" to be off putting? I didn't care. This was a desperation move. I liked a few more of her photos for good measure and then gave my phone a rest. Any excessive use of my iPhone was taxing due to the fickle reception. So, I didn't obsess over her pictures like I likely would have under normal circumstances. Plus Christmas was around the corner.

Christmas morning we had our traditional breakfast of egg McMuffins and orange juice. Like I did every year, I received more books than most people had ever owned in their lives. We exchanged sentimental gifts, and as always some tears made an appearance.

After another week or so of movie watching and frequent naps, I returned home, back to reality.

Child had not followed me back on Instagram. I really wasn't too downtrodden because I knew she had a boyfriend. Why would she follow me back, or like my pictures? She probably didn't even know who I was. Not much changed in the next month or so besides the ushering in of 2014. My life had found some traces of routine. I was working, writing, playing in two basketball leagues and going out on the occasional date or casual hang out. Life was good. I was still recovering from the assorted setbacks of 2013, but I was happy. I didn't think much of Child. We didn't run in the same circles, and all I saw of her was the occasional post that was usually a well-edited picture of her and her splendid boyfriend doing something cute. It was almost like a celebrity crush. I knew nothing about her, certainly would never have her, but was still intrigued by her every move.

On the first day of February Child started following me on Instagram. This may sound about as inconsequential and trivial as a celebrity retweeting something you posted online. But for me it spoke volumes. She must have looked through my pictures and found me at least somewhat attractive or interesting. Was she still with her boyfriend? I quickly checked her account, but her last photo was with him. Maybe she was just being nice, and hadn't gotten around to following me before. She seemed like the type of person to just be genuinely warm to everyone. So, again I didn't think much about it. I was excited, but realistic. It was like getting a kiss on the cheek from Jennifer Anniston. It is flattering and exciting, but you know it doesn't really mean anything. And it certainly means more to you than it does to her. Nevertheless I smiled and counted myself lucky.

The following Thursday I went to Pizza Pie Café with Bryce. We piled up our plates with mediocre slices from the buffet and talked about Bryce's recent participation in a medical experiment. He couldn't feel cold on his skin anymore. He proved this to me by putting a handful of ice on his face. I guess having a numb face for a few days isn't so bad for $1,400. We both went back for seconds and thirds and continued gabbing about girls and money.

I had a slice of jalapeño pizza in my hand when I saw my phone on the table vibrate. It was Lauren. What on earth could she want? We were the type of friends that didn't talk and didn't hang out. We just happened to have a lot of mutual friends, so we were cordial and occasionally chummy when we saw each other.

"Hello"

"Hey Taylor, how you doing?"

"Good, what's up Lauren?"

Bryce, almost unaware that I was even on the phone, continued to inhale pasta while little kids noisily ran around our table.

"Hey, are you dating anyone right now?"

"Um, no...why?"

"Well, I have a friend that thinks you are cute."

"Who?"

"Well I don't know if you know her, but you guys follow each other on Instagram."

Could it be? No. There's no way.

"Who is it Lauren?"

"Her name is Christy."

"You're kidding me."

"No I'm not, why do you say that?"

"Um cause I love her. But wait, doesn't she have a boyfriend?"

"They just broke up"

Our conversation ended and Lauren texted me Child's number with the additional knowledge that she was expecting my text. I hung up and had a ridiculous smile. I explained to Bryce who she was, and how things had come together. He was less interested in the romantic details; he just wanted to see a picture. So, I showed him her Instagram account and he made all the appropriate sounds that guys make when they see a beautiful woman, and simply don't have any actual words.

I decided to wait until later that night to send my first strategic text. This was the big leagues. I felt like a medieval peasant that had just been invited to dine with the newly single queen; my RSVP had to be grandiloquent. A few hours later I started composing my first text to Child. I said, "Hey Christy, this is Taylor Church. Lauren gave me your number. Hopefully she wasn't just playing a cruel trick on me. But if she wasn't, I would love to take you out sometime, and more formally make your fine acquaintance."

I was rather impressed with my candor and playfulness. She would have no choice but to love that text. She quickly responded saying, "Hey hey! Noo she wasn't playing a cruel trick on you! I think that sounds lovely."

Part of me flushed with confidence thinking I had it in the bag, but the other part of me was terribly uncertain. We made a date for the following Thursday. Planning for an entire week ahead was dangerous. It gave her eons of time to have something else come up. For all I knew she might get back together with her boyfriend or meet someone entirely new within a seven day period. But her work schedule was inhuman and it was her only window that week. So, I took what I could get and planned for success.

Throughout the week we texted almost every day and discussed our forthcoming date. She had to be at work at four o'clock in the morning so it would have to be an early night on the town. Wednesday night we were talking and realized that I had a basketball game, and would not be able to pick her up until ten-thirty or so. I was afraid we would have to postpone our date, but I knew that would not be the smart thing to do. As I had predicted she suggested maybe we try another night. I responded with the suggestion that we simply meet at her place, talk, get to know each other a little better and call it a "warm-up date." To my surprise, she loved the idea.

This was good and bad. I didn't have to impress her off the bat with my table manners or knowledge of delectable cuisines. But I had to show up with sparkling and refreshing conversation. We would only be chatting for forty-five minutes at the max, so I couldn't afford to have any lulls, stutters or mispronunciations. I had to come across intelligent without being ostentatious. I had to be flirtatious without being creepy or overzealous. It was a fine balance, a balance I was usually comfortable with. But I was starting to feel the pressure that there was not a single inch designated for error.

When my basketball game ended it was roughly ten o'clock. I gave out the appropriate amounts of high fives and job-well-done pats, and sprinted to the locker room to primp myself. Child warned me that she had been moving her sister, so she would be in moving clothes and not especially made up. Since I was still covered in perspiration I would also not be my most presentable self. But I had to look semi-dashing, it was my first impression and I had to leave a mark, a red-carpet sort of indent.

I headed north to her apartment complex. She lived right next to a Wal-Mart and a baseball field. I was nervous. It lightly drizzled the whole way up and thoughts were everywhere. I tried not to overthink things, but that effort was in vain from the onset. She was too much; too beautiful, too sanguine, too fantastic.

She was otherworldly. But as I parked I gave myself a little pep talk, reminding my inner self that I was in fact the man, and that Child actually had wanted to meet me.

I walked around searching for her apartment number. I didn't want to call her and admit that I was lost, but I couldn't find the elusive 102A. I finally accosted a couple carrying in groceries, "Do you guys know where 102A is?"

"Ya, it's right there" they pointed. I was four feet away from the threshold. The time had arrived to meet this girl. But she was not a girl, she was a lady. The difference between the two is not defined by age, but by an ineffable quality of grace and aplomb.

I knocked on the door wondering if she would answer or a roommate. The door waved open slowly and there she was. She was so petit it flirted with perfection. She looked up to me and said "You found it!" Apparently her address was not always GPS friendly. We hugged and I knew the night would be enjoyable.

We walked inside and sat down on her couch. I was immediately aware of two things. First she had no roommates, and second her apartment was absolutely immaculate. Not only was there not a trace of clutter, it also had all the frills and décor of a fine 17th century royal chamber. Child collected antiques, but not the raggedy kind you find in grungy pawn shops. Her stuff was classy. It looked like she had robbed a museum. I was experiencing sensory overload. Not only was her home drenched in chic fanciness, but Child herself seemed to glisten with raw beauty.

Soon after we commenced speaking I knew something was right. So often on dates, especially first dates the conversation is not organic, but characterized by bursts of questions and attempts at humor. Our words seemed to be playing together like two little kids in a sandbox. It was natural and easy, almost familiar. I was funny and clever without even trying. She was charming and cute. What really stood out to me were her books. I am a bibliophile, and this makes dating hard since there is a vile amount of people in this world that don't love literature or worse, don't read at all. Some girls I have courted when asked about the last book they have read have had to think back years to when they were last assigned to read *Of Mice and Men* in high school. This is depressing. On the flip side, when a girl has multiple copies of *Anna Karenina* visible from one sitting position, things start to look up.

Child had a few fastidiously stacked piles of books in her front room, but once the topic turned to tomes she got excited and led me to her room where her entire collection rested. I sat on the corner of the bed, while she kneeled next to me grabbing book after book, showing me her notes and asking me if I had read certain titles. This was the sexiest thing I had seen in a while. A lower-caliber girl could have easily seduced me with glib talk about Tolstoy and author's notes. But an upper echelon girl like Child, forget about it. She had me. It was over. She had played her cards just right, but the best part was she did it effortlessly. It wasn't as if she was a lucky gambler who happened to have a good hand. She was an experienced card-dealer that did not have to put on an act. I was a ten year old boy hanging out with his crush; I was deeply and irreversibly smitten.

Our dialogue returned to the living room on the couch where our legs touched. You could tell Child was old-fashioned. We would not be kissing that night, or even the next, but that was okay.

We covered an amazing amount of topics in two hours. We discussed our favorite tennis players, our siblings and our disdain for non-readers. She was genuinely interested in my sentences and stories, and for a change I sincerely cared about the things she had to say. Far too often on a date I found myself daydreaming while a girl was talking. I would listen just enough to insert timely "oh wow's" or "oh my gosh's." When you have made up your mind to not ever see someone again it is terribly difficult to care about the scuttlebutt in their office, or the fact that their roommate "never does the dishes." But Child seemed to spew knowledge from her mouth. Everything she said was elegant and insightful. I listened like I would have a comprehensive final exam on the matter the following day. I almost took notes.

It was nearing one o'clock in the morning and Child had to be awake in two hours. Her eyes started to get heavy as if a little fairy was placing quarters on her eyelids. Her eyes, however, were huge, so I guess they might have been fifty-cent pieces. She wasn't going to ask me to leave, but I could tell she was getting tired and quietly worried about being able to function the next day at work. I slowly stood up, motioning that it was probably time to go.

Before I even got to the door she started thanking me for coming. Most girls have the decency to thank a man for his efforts at the end of the night, but you can often hear the monotony of the ritual in their voice. Child was strangely sincere. She thanked me for making the drive, talking with her and for making her laugh. Then we hugged for the second time ever, this time a little longer, with a little more meaning. I pivoted toward the door and we locked eyes. I smiled the kind of smile that does not reveal teeth, but reveals much more. She reciprocated with an up curve of the mouth that rippled over my entire body. I said goodnight and walked out. The second the door was shut an enormous smile, the kind that forces a tiny giggle out of your throat swept across my face. I walked to my car not knowing what would happen, but not caring. Just knowing that a girl like this existed and actually wanted to spend time with me had completely renewed my damaged faith in women and love. The rain persisted, as did my smile the whole way home.

The End